Tom Sheppard

Cover Art: © 2017 Thomas K Sheppard, includes "Red paint tray" © 2017 @ Irochka, Used with permission by arrangement with DepositPhotos.com

Copyright © 2017 Thomas K Sheppard and A+ Results, LLC
All rights reserved

ISBN: 1979467544
ISBN-13: 9781979467544

## DEDICATION

For my family: My wife Angela, my children Rachel, TK, Ben, Janel, Rebekah and especially Jillian and Tony who made conscious decisions to join this family. I have used both the science and the art of project management to provide for their well-being for many years now.

# CONTENTS

Dedication ..................................................................................... iii
Contents ......................................................................................... v
Acknowledegments ..................................................................... viii
Preface: Why I Wrote This Book ................................................ ix
Chapter 1: Are You a Project Manager? ..................................... 1
Chapter 2: Art Versus Science .................................................... 6
Chapter 3: Project Leadership .................................................. 15
Chapter 4: Managing Risks and Issues ..................................... 19
Chapter 5: Effective Project Failure ......................................... 25
Chapter 6: Ask the Right Questions ......................................... 29
Chapter 7: The Impacts of Change ........................................... 33
Chapter 8: Hiring Right ............................................................. 37
Chapter 9: Motivating Others ................................................... 43
Chapter 10: Office Politics ........................................................ 56
Chapter 11: The Laws of Power for the PM ............................. 66
Chapter 12: Corporate Culture Traps ....................................... 72
Chapter 13: Project Impacts ...................................................... 76
Chapter 14: Constructive Conflict ............................................ 80
Chapter 14: Using Stress ............................................................ 85
Chapter 15: Persuasion .............................................................. 89
Chapter 16: Negotiation .......................................................... 102
Chapter 17: Measurement ....................................................... 108
Chapter 18: Technical Skills .................................................... 113
Chapter 19: Brand Management ............................................. 120
Chapter 20: The Wrong PM for the Job ................................. 124
Chapter 21: Applying the 80/20 Rule ..................................... 129
Relevant Reading ..................................................................... 140

About the Author ................................................................ 150
Other Titles by Tom Sheppard ...................................... 152

# ACKNOWLEDEGMENTS

While earning my Masters in Project Management at Western Carolina University I had the pleasure to work with, and be taught by James P Lewis and John R Adams. These two men designed the curriculum we studied. The art and the science of project management were intermingled in their design. I have found both aspects of project management to be essential to my success as a project manager and am grateful for their wisdom and insight in their instruction.

William (Bill) Taggart taught me a lot about the art of project management in the brief time I worked for him. This manuscript was nearly complete and this acknowledgement was already written when I learned of his sudden death a short while ago. May he rest in peace.

My thanks to Jeffrey Pace, PMP and Rosemary Barrett. My colleagues had the patience to read my manuscript and offer helpful suggestions.

Lastly, I would like to acknowledge my colleague Susan Staples and the other project managers who worked with me on a core software systems replacement project. They reaffirmed for me the distinction between truly successful, powerful, effective project managers and all the rest. They epitomized the former and we fired several of the latter.

# PREFACE: WHY I WROTE THIS BOOK

I have been managing large ($10mm+), high-risk, high-profile projects in the financial services sector of the US for many years now. During that time I have hired and fired a number of project managers who came to work with me. I took note of the reasons why some of these experienced project managers failed while others succeeded, along with me.

When I weeded out those few who had insufficient mastery of the science of project management I found that what those who failed universally lacked was sufficient skill in the art of project management.

I took it upon myself to find a good book or two which I could point people at to help them improve these critical skills. What I found surprised and disappointed me.

While project management literature abounds with books, courses, degrees and certifications that teach the science of project management, there is almost nothing out there that actually addresses the critical, soft-skills, that comprise the art of project management.

There is little I can say about the science of project management which has not been said and perhaps explained beyond my abilities. The most I can say about the science is that the building of task chains of successors and dependents is utterly indispensable for the peace of mind of every project manager.

However, there is much I can share about the art of project management. To be clear, there is a distinct difference between the art of project management and flying by the seat of your pants. The art of project management is worthless by itself. To work, it must be founded firmly on the proper application of the science of project management.

The art of PM is fundamentally about leadership, motivation and relationship management.

Leading from the middle. Managing upward, sideways and downward. It is about getting others to want to do what you need them to do, when you need them to do it.

It is relatively easy to "lead" and "motivate" when we hold a position of organizational authority over others. They will follow directions and pretend to be enthusiastic or motivated when we have the power to fire them at will.

True leadership elicits motivation without using the fear of dismissal. The art of PM comes into play most often when the PM has to work in a matrix organization where s/he holds little or no formal authority and has only the power of his expertise to garner respect and obedience.

Reading this book will not give you all the answers about the art of project management. This is a book, not an encyclopedia. However, it will give you a good start and, I hope, a reading list for further study and development of your skills.

On the other hand, this book may simply terrify you and make you decide to limit your ambitions as a project manager to what you can do with the science and very little use of the art of project management. That too is a legitimate outcome.

Enjoy,
Tom Sheppard
2017

© 2017 by Sergey Nivens, Used with Permission through DepositPhotos.com

# CHAPTER 1: ARE YOU A PROJECT MANAGER?

"We will either find a way, or make one."

Hannibal

In the most exact sense of the word, anyone who is managing a project (a collection of tasks with a collective objective, finite duration and non-repetitive purpose) can be called a project manager, whether or not they hold that title.

However, I have found there is a great deal of difference between skills and art needed by a manager who runs a project inside of his or her department, or a line of business leader who oversees a project in their division or company versus a project manager who holds no direct authority over any one business unit and yet is tasked with successfully carrying out a project which crosses organizational boundaries.

The skillful project manager will know how to do pretty much everything a business line leader knows. However, where the business line leader may enjoy coming to work each day and pushing his or her unit toward better and better performance, the skillful project manager craves the challenge of building that performance from zero, or jumping it forward by an order of magnitude over what has been happening before.

The differences between a project manager and an operations manager became painfully clear to me while working for a major national bank in the US.

I was tasked to drive the project to implement their operational risk management system, which I did. Once it was operational, they asked me to run it for a while to continue to tune the system. To be clear, when I say system, I refer to processes carried out by people and facilitated by appropriate automation.

I ran the system for about a year after implementation. Near the end of that year, I sat down opposite the system owner and told him he needed to fire me and hire a real operations manager.

You might be able to imagine how shocked he was to hear me say that he should fire me.

I explained, "Project managers and operations managers have a lot of the same skills, however they have different dispositions which dramatically affect how they use those skills. Project management is about building things. Operations management is about maintaining things and fine tuning things." I concluded by telling him, "Project management gets me up in the morning. Operations management keeps me up at night. I am tired of not being able to go to sleep in the evening and not wanting to get up in the morning."

Although I have run teams who extended membership numbered in the hundreds, I have no burning desire to run a department of hundreds of people. I have successfully run departments, with all their attendant tasks and challenges and managed yearly budgets for them which ran into the millions. But, after successfully building the team to have their work more than offset their budgetary expenses year after year, I was ready to move on to something new and different, rather than just a larger version of the same thing.

If that resonates with you, then you may have the disposition to be a project manager. But wait, there's more!

When a project is run by a line manager or a department head, even if it crosses organizational boundaries, the project leader has positional authority available to overcome resistance and proprietary resources to get the work done by command.

When a project manager must operate in a matrixed management structure, s/he has little or no positional authority or proprietary resources. Absent the crutches available to a line manager, the matrixed project manager must learn real, genuine leadership skills in order to motivate people to do what needs to be done. The power play of relying on the organizational authority of the project sponsor is the course of last resort for a project manager, and relying upon it reveals the lack of actual authority the project manager holds. It is the same as "going over someone's head", and it can end very badly for everyone when a powerful manager is forced to take a stand between a project manager and a department head.

In contrast with this risk that project managers in matrixed roles face, the department head who is acting as a project manager has clearly defined boundaries of power and authority and can tell another manager to "do it because I said so," and get away with it. That is a power play that a matrixed project manager can only take at great personal risk, to order actions on his or her own authority.

And yet, the skillful project manager will know when to overreach beyond their official authority and put themselves at risk of dismissal in order to deliver the results the business needs.

Call me a project management snob if you will, but until you have run a project in a matrixed environment, I don't think you have really experienced the meat of project management, regardless of what title you held. Up until then, you have been able to rely almost wholly upon the science of project management, regardless of how big the project was.

This book will help any prospective or actual manager to learn some skills that will serve them well. However, this book is not written for them. If you fall in that group and you benefit from this, then that is wonderful. This book was written specifically for project managers who have to run high-risk, big-budget, large-team projects in a matrixed management environment where they have little to no positional authority. In these projects, you must succeed or fail based on your expertise coupled with your personal leadership skills, your charismatic authority.

Your charismatic authority is based on your personal abilities, people skills, and expertise which inspire people to respect you and desire to do what you ask of them.

This is not to imply that to succeed you must transform yourself into some sort of Svengali who seduces, dominates or exploits people. Rather, it means you must both possess and project attributes, knowledge and abilities which inspire confidence. And, you must be able to use and project them in ways which do not automatically threaten the authority and leadership of others.

When you possess these leadership abilities, it is no small feat to exercise them without making others feel threatened. Your natural confidence may come across as arrogance or aggressiveness. Your proven performance may make others look bad by comparison. All these factors may inspire some to resent, oppose and even undermine you personally and professionally.

Charismatic authority is not some mystical power that you are either born with or you will never have it. While it is true that some will never be able to muster even a spark of charismatic authority, and others will burn with it like a floodlight in the night, the reality is that most of us fall between those two extremes. Because of that, we can develop charismatic authority through knowledge and thoughtful, diligent effort.

As a Mormon Missionary in South America and as a Marine Non-Commissioned Officer (NCO) I learned some basics about leadership and the ability to motivate others.

As a missionary and from subsequent roles as a volunteer leader in a voluntary organization I learned how to lead and motivate without the ability to enforce my will.

As a Marine NCO I learned that using your authority to enforce your will is a quick way to demoralize those you lead and to risk far worse than disrespect at their hands when the opportunity might be presented.

As a manager and as a project manager in defense contracting, systems development, financial services and real estate investing I have honed my skills and refined my knowledge of how to intelligently apply what I know while building high performing teams.

My own development of charismatic authority has not been a straight line, and it has not led to some national or international platform where thousands hear me and follow my directions. If that sort of power is where you want to go, then this is not the lesson book for you. However, if you want to learn how to really lead people to their own peak performance as individuals and teams to deliver extraordinary results in projects and have them willing to work with you again, then I can teach you how to do that because that is what skillful project managers do. And, they do it on project after project. It is no flash-in-the-pan or luck.

If that is what you want and are willing to pay for it with intelligent actions, hard work and iron-willed self-discipline, then read on and learn how to become a truly skillful project manager.

© Copyright 2017 by @ Iurii, Image used with permission through DepositPhotos.com

## CHAPTER 2: ART VERSUS SCIENCE

*"How often people speak of art and science as though they were two entirely different things, with no interconnection. That is all wrong. The true artist is quite rational as well as imaginative and knows what he is doing; if he does not, his art suffers. The true scientist is quite imaginative as well as rational, and sometimes leaps to solutions where reason can follow only slowly; if he does not, his science suffers."*

Isaac Asimov

As a discipline, project management finds its greatest adherents in the construction and software development industries. Because both of these industries are rather technical in their nature, this means that the majority of project managers tend to be technicians, or like myself, have technical roots.

Anyone who has worked in a technical discipline knows that techies often lack highly refined social skills. They are generally more comfortable working with things and shaping things to their will. They tend to shy away from all that "touchy-feely" stuff like relationship management.

As a result of this technical influence pervading the lives of project managers, most are far more comfortable learning and practicing the science of project management. Discussions of the art of project management tend to veer back into the realm of the science.

For instance, ask an experienced project manager about the art of estimation and s/he may get very animated on the topic, throwing several examples of techniques they use to get more accurate estimates. The same thing may happen when you talk about building project schedules or stakeholder responsibility (RACI) charts. Unfortunately, the reality is that estimating, scheduling building, and RACI development are all within the realm of the science of project management. Each of them relies heavily upon clear, repeatable, processes which yield relatively predictable outcomes.

In essence, the science of project management versus the art of project management can be compared to a draftsman's rendering of an object with all its notations of dimensions and other properties compared with an artist's rendering of the same object in living color and with their interpretation thrown in. Both figures have an element of beauty and elegance. The draftsman's rendering, however, can readily be duplicated by countless other draftsmen around the world, simply by following the rules of drafting. In contrast, the artist's rendering is unlikely to be duplicated exactly, and will more likely reflect the views of the subsequent artist. Only the forger seeks to utterly duplicate the masterpiece.

This difference between the "touchy-feeley" art of project management and the cold, hard science of project management tends to make most project managers uncomfortable, because of their technical (thing-oriented) backgrounds. Unfortunately for most project managers, the science of project management will only take you so far. It is the art of project management that will lift you from the mass of ordinary project managers into the more rarified atmosphere of truly skillful project managers.

Because of this relative level of comfort, there is a wealth of literature and training out there on the science of project management. However, there is a near total absence of anything at all that is focused on the art of project management.

Scott Berkun in 2005 published a book titled, *The Art of Project Management*. Unfortunately, while he does hit on some aspects of the art of project management, too often he slides back into the topics of the science of project management. In fact, when I searched Amazon's book listings using the phrase "art of project management" although I was returned a list of more than 2,000 titles, after the first three, all of them were about the science of project management and various project methodologies. Scott Berkun had the first and second slots, with the emphasis on getting things done, while the third was a book by David Allen and James Fallows titled *Getting Things Done: The Art of Stress-Free Productivity*. It has been my experience that books on productivity focus on efficiency. And, efficiency is about science.

Stephen R Covey in his book *The 7 Habits of Highly Effective People* makes the point that when it comes to dealing with people you usually have to choose between being efficient and being effective. This idea strikes most techies as utter rubbish. They are accustomed to very efficient and effective communications with other techies on a daily basis. Their conversations tend to be short, highly focused, filled with jargon which works as a shorthand for communications between techies. While all that is true, then ask them about how good a communicator their spouse or parents think they are. In most cases, there is an uncomfortable pause followed by an admission or an excuse. Looking past the admissions and excuses reveals that most techies are barely adequate to lousy communicators once they move outside of their techie zone of comfort with other techies.

In fact, the entire job category of business analysts has been created in an attempt to find and cultivate people with the ability to bridge the gap between geek-speak and business-speak. However, business analysts operate at the level of requirements elucidation, not managing large, high-risk, high-profile projects. There is a career path that leads from business analysis into project management. Unfortunately, it usually does not involve enough mastery of the science of project management to allow the ambitious business analyst to develop their skills in both the art and science of project management to the levels needed to successfully manage large, high-profile, high-risk projects.

Back to my point. Project management books about efficiency, metrics, and methodologies are books about the science of project management. So, if you want to learn about the art of project management, that leaves just Mr. Berkun's books and mine. And, his are diluted by digressions into the science, pretending it is art.

The science of project management is all about math, processes, checklists, metrics, measurements, systems, tools and methodologies. All of which tend to be highly predictable and pretty uniformly repeatable by different people in different environments.

The nature of the science of project management makes it the easiest aspects of the business to teach. And, many who bear the title of project manager and project coordinator or project administrator are experts in the science of project management. And yet, these same project management experts, when given a large, high-risk, high-profile project do everything right according the science, and fail spectacularly.

When projects are small and middling sized (< $10mm), the science alone is often sufficient to carry the project manager to success. However, the larger the project, the greater becomes the influence of the human element. And, when humanity and science mix it up, science doesn't stand a chance by itself.

The human factor becomes even more important when the focus of the project relies upon knowledge work instead of straightforward, manual labor.

Frederick Taylor kicked off the study of making manual labor processes efficient with his time and motion studies back in the 1880's and 1890's. His principles of scientific management, or Taylorism, are still tremendously important when you need to optimize manual processes. But, how can you optimize processes that are executed inside the mind and produce inherently creative outputs such as computer programs, organizational design, management consulting, financial analyses, requirements development, etc.?

The science of project management leverages principles of

scientific management. Those principles are best applied when the project manager is primarily dealing with things. The art of project management, and the underlying principles of that art are best applied when the project manager is primarily dealing with people, particularly with powerful individuals and small groups of people.

However, the skillful and successful project manager has a superior level of mastery over both the science and the art of project management. Those masteries are essential for any PM tasked with managing high-risk, high-profile projects, especially when intellectual capital is the primary building ingredient.

A well-built project plan is a plan with tasks that have realistic durations or effort estimates, and fully articulated relationships with all other tasks in the plan.

There is little I can say about the science of project management which has not been said and perhaps explained beyond my abilities. The most I can say about the science is that the building of task chains of successors and dependents is utterly indispensable for the peace of mind of every project manager.

Elyhu Goldrat, in his book *The Critical Chain*, teaches the importance of understanding all the task chains in a project, not just paying attention to the critical path. Building the task chains in a project is heavily reliant on the science of project management.

Building tasks with realistic duration or effort estimates and understanding predecessor and successor tasks, and how they depend upon one another are critical to building a realistic, attainable project plan. They are also indispensable to finding ways to compress a project plan as much as possible to deliver a project in a time frame which makes it viable for a business to fund and support. It is in building these elements of a project plan that the science of project management delivers its greatest value, and a correct linkage of all the tasks from one end of the project to another is the insurance against failure that the science of project management can deliver.

All other aspects of the science of project management, resource leveling, cost estimation, project evaluation, project controls, etc., are meaningless, time-consuming activities without the presence of a well-built project plan.

The PMBOK® (Project Management Body of Knowledge) is a great resource for project managers. But, it is just that, a resource.

Project management methodologies such as Lean, Six Sigma, Agile, etc. are all resources too. They are tools in the toolbox of an expert PM. But, they are no substitute for excellent project management skills. The skilled PM does not allow himself to become the mindless proselyting of any one PM methodology. The skilled PM has these methodologies in her toolbox and applies them as appropriate to each part of each project.

The ability to appropriately and intelligently apply different methodologies, even within the same project is the beginning of the art of project management which a skilled PM must master.

Management guru Tom Peters, in an essay entitled *Pursuing the Perfect Project Manager* (© 1991 TPG Communications) explains eight things that a skillful project manager must balance in order to succeed:

1. **Total ego/no ego.** To succeed, project managers must be consumed by the project; the best invest their egos in the job and "become" their projects, sometimes for years. Yet project managers must also have no ego at all. They deal with numerous, diverse outsiders and insiders, whom they can hardly "command." (They neither have formal authority, nor even a clear understanding of what many of the others are up to.) Contributors must have their own high ego involvement—which means the project manager must be expert at letting others take full credit for what they've done and a disproportionate share of the kudos for overall success.
2. **Autocrat/delegator.** When the chips are down, the project manager has got to issue the orders, fast—e.g., when the lights go out in the conference center, with 5,000 people streaming in. On the other hand, she or he needs to be a masterful delegator: In that crisis when the lights go out, lighting experts should "own the problem" and have

taken the initiative to deal with the situation before the chief ever became aware of it.

3. **Leader/manager.** Today's project managers, more so than in traditional settings, are only as good as their teammates' commitment, energy and diverse skills. So project managers must be leaders—visionaries and invigorators. On the other hand, "management" means being expert at the mechanics. Stellar project bosses match a passion for inspiring others with a love for the nuts and bolts of the job.

4. **Tolerate ambiguity/pursue perfection.** The essence of complex project is ambiguity. The only "for sure" is the unexpected. Effective project managers handle equivocality with elan and a sense of humor. But they must have equal zeal for the tidy. The downfall of botched projects is most often a trifle—e.g., overlooking bus transportation to a special event for 500 convention attendees.

5. **Oral/written.** Most people have either an oral or a "put it in writing" bias. Top project managers must have both. They are wrong to insist upon an "audit trail" of memos to document every this or that; dealing orally, on the fly, must come easily. However, project managers must also be compulsive about the written master plan and the daily "to-do list."

6. **Acknowledge complexity/champion simplicity.** Nothing is more complex than a sophisticated, multi-organization project. Effective project managers must juggle a thousand balls—of differing (and ever changing!) shapes and sizes. On the other hand, they must be "Keep It Simple, Stupid" fanatics—making sure that a few, essential values dominate the organization (e.g., nobody misses the 7 a.m. Monday meeting).

7. **Think big/think small.** Project managers must appreciate forests and trees. Those fixated with the "big picture" will come a cropper over details. Yet "god-is-in-the-details" project managers may miss the main point. Success means seeing the relationship of the tiny to the large, the large to the tiny—at every moment.

8. **Impatient/patient.** Project managers must be "action fanatics": Get on with it; don't dwell on yesterday's bobbles. At the same time, they run a network with fragile egos, multiple cultures and complex relationships. Of course, project managers don't "run" networks at all—they are, at most, first among equals. Forget the word "subcontractor"—substitute "co-contractor." Think the same way about each member of a project team. When one deals with co-equals, devoting lots of time to "relationship building" becomes as important as impatiently pushing for action.

**The big consulting companies** (e.g., PWC, D&T, E&Y, Accenture, KPMG and others) have figured out the art and science divide of projects in their own way. They usually keep the two separate.

Management consulting companies, when seeking an engagement first send in a team that understands business-speak and have mastered the arts of persuasion and negotiation. The lead team are, more or less, marketers. Their job is to build the case that the business needs the project and that their team is able to successfully deliver the project.

Once the artists of communication and persuasion have sealed the deal, they bring in a team of technologists, usually led by a member of the lead team, to execute the science of project management. If the technical project leader gets into trouble, s/he brings in the member of the lead team to soothe the ruffled feathers of the corporate management and allow the technical team to continue their work.

Unfortunately, this model is not optimized for success because the technical lead is unable to exercise true leadership, either through inability or lack of training / experience, and the business lead lacks the technical experience to know when the technologists are using smoke screens to hide what it really happening. The optimal solution for success is to have a skillful project manager who is experienced in both the art and science of project management. S/he has enough technical knowledge to see past the diversionary tactics of the technologists along with enough business acumen to see through the same efforts on the business side, and has the leadership and communication skills necessary to manage the corporate bosses effectively so that the smoke is cleared away and the job gets done, without having to relinquish leadership roles to a business lead whose very presence tends to undermine the confidence of management in the project manager.

These consulting firms keep the two roles separate simply because it is so hard to find project managers who are skillful in both the art and the science of project manager. It is easier to cultivate the skills separately, in different individuals, and keep the birds of a feather together. As a result, their hiring and execution models typically do not recruit or exploit skillful project managers. The net effect of this is that costs to business clients tend to exceed estimates and it takes longer to implement the desired project than what the marketing team got management to buy off on. That outcome is not deliberate, but it does fatten the bottom line of the consulting companies.

My experience is that these skillful project managers who have mastered both the art and the science of project management are out there in the marketplace. Occasionally, they get the chance to really show their stuff. However, in most cases, businesses have come to believe the model of the consulting companies and accept that the ability to master both doesn't exist in the workforce. Because of that bias, these skillful project managers are typically working on projects well below their capacity, or they have abandoned hope of working to their full capacity and gone over wholly to the management consulting arena. Either way, they have surrendered to one side or another, and have become victims of a defective, mediocre industry model.

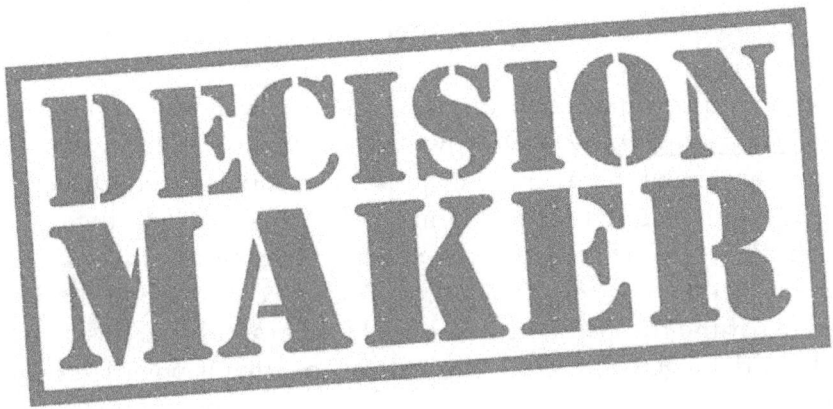

© Copyright 2017 by @ chrisdorney, Image used with permission through DepositPhotos.com

## CHAPTER 3: PROJECT LEADERSHIP

"**Management is doing things right. Leadership is doing the right things.**"

Peter Drucker

Never take your position for granted. Regardless of whatever assurances or guarantees you may have been given, your charter can be revoked in an instant and you will find yourself suddenly standing on the curb, your name plate in a box at your feet, wondering how you went from prestige and power to penury.

Master your emotions – do not ever respond to events from a base of emotion. Emotion will always betray you. If you react in anger, then you are out of control. If you react in sorrow and tears, then you are weak. In either case, you are unsteady and unreliable. Or at least so your enemies will cast your emotional reactions.

And you will have enemies. In any project the project manager will have enemies, whether you have done anything overt to deserve them or not. Your enemies will first be among those who oppose the project. Second they will be among those who support the project, but are certain they can lead it better than you.

Your enemies will use every and any means at their disposal to thwart you or remove you. If you don't protect yourself, your project, and your project team, your enemies will drive you out.

_Downward Leadership_ - My own philosophy of leadership is primarily shaped by my training as a Noncommissioned Offcer (NCO) in the United States Marine Corps. As an NCO I was taught that I had exactly two directives. The first directive is to accomplish the mission. The second directive is to see to the welfare of the troops. Anytime I could accomplish the mission without damaging the welfare of the troops, that is what I should do.

In civilian life as a manager and particularly as a project manager I have found these two maxims to be invaluable tools of leadership.

Regardless of what is going on, you must always keep in mind what is the mission and determine what must be done to accomplish it. Aside from your own mind, the greatest tool you have available to you to accomplish that mission is your project team, your troops. If you take care of your team, they will take care of you. And when you don't needlessly, or wantonly squander their well-being, they will be willing to sacrifice their well-being to help you accomplish the mission.

This two-way street of management and leadership has been proven by my experiences time and again. Keeping these dictums in mind, I have consistently built high-performing teams on every project I managed and in every business unit I have managed.

Leadership on large, high-risk, high-profile projects requires 360 degree leadership. The skillful PM not only knows how to lead his or her project team, s/he knows how to lead from the middle by getting higher level managers to deliver what you want and need as well as to get your peers, those at the same organizational level to follow your lead and give you what you need, when you need it.

*Upward Leadership* – The first rule of upward management is to never outshine the boss. Always try to make the boss look good to his or her boss(es).

The second rule is related to the first rule – Never surprise your boss. Good or bad, when you announce something in a meeting that you didn't already discuss with your boss, you are making the boss look bad. You should always make it appear like your boss is fully on top of everything of consequence that is happening in your space. The best way to do that, is to make it true.

*Lateral Leadership* – The first rule off lateral management is that you can always catch more flies with honey than you can with vinegar. By deliberately setting up win-win situations and doing things to make your peers look good, you employ one of the most important rules of persuasion, the principle of reciprocity. In other words, you helping them makes them feel the need to return the favor.

However, reciprocity in too large doses will backfire and inspire those who owe you to bury you instead of helping you. Remember, "Men are more ready to repay an injury than a benefit, because gratitude is a burden and revenge a pleasure." TACITUS, c. A.D. 55-120. And, when a debt of gratitude becomes a burden, the easiest way to cancel the debt is to kill the lender.

> **"Gratitude is a burden and revenge a pleasure,"**
> Tacitus circa AD 55-120

In today's world killing the lender doesn't work too well to cancel a debt. However, in the Middle Ages, nobles and Kings often incurred significant debts to fund wars. The most common lenders were Jews. This was because charging interest was considered usury and Christian clerics deemed usury was a sin. Jews did not support that interpretation of scripture and were unimpeded by divine laws in becoming lenders and charging interest.

At various times, however, the Christian nobles who had

borrowed to fund wars or other efforts found their debts to be inconvenient. All too often they would then foment anti-Jewish sentiment and generate a violent pogrom of killing Jews, in the course of which not only would these nobles manage to kill their lender(s) but they would also loot and pillage their lenders so that the debt was both cancelled and the debtor enriched by the theft of the worldly goods of the dead lender.

The debts of gratitude you might manage to incur as a project manager can largely be eliminated if your project is cancelled or you are fired, or both. Your debtor has, in effect, killed you to cancel the debt. Once you are outside the organization, or out of favor, it is easy for the debtor to pretend to help you, while actually doing nothing.

Above all else, the skillful project manager provides leadership that is not partisan to one faction of the organization or even to a given solution to the business problem being addressed. By remaining uncompromised by factionalism, and focused on the big picture, the skillful project manager leads the project to successfully navigate the big risks which would destroy the project from the outside. By exerting sufficient attention to detail, the skillful project manager resolves issues so that they don't destroy the project from the inside.

The Art of Project Management

© Copyright 2017 by almagami, Image used with permission through DepositPhotos.com

## CHAPTER 4: MANAGING RISKS AND ISSUES

**"Risk comes from not knowing what you're doing."**
Warren Buffett

The skillful project manager understands the difference between risks and issues and knows how to properly foresee and manage both.

Ultimately, project management is all about risk management. Especially for large, complex projects, each project is a microcosm of the business itself, and incorporates nearly all the same risks as the business itself lives with.

My specialty is for large ($10mm+) projects in the financial services sector. Each project I manage has elements of regulatory risk, market risk, credit risk, and operational risk. These are all the same risks which my client companies face every day. They typically have risk management departments where risk professionals study every aspect of the business to calculate their exposure to various risks and to push the company to take appropriate steps to manage their risks.

The skillful project manager is as responsible for managing all these risks for the project as the CEO is for the whole company. Neither the successful CEO, nor the skillful PM attempt to manage all these risks themselves. However, they both must have a decent working knowledge of these risks and be able to take measures to monitor and manage them.

When it comes to risk management, the single most important skill the project manager needs is the ability to constantly envision problems before they arrive. One of my mentors referred to this skill as "looking over the horizon," or "seeing around corners" to anticipate what is coming next.

The average chess player thinks just 3 moves ahead. A very good chess player envisions 5 to 8 moves ahead. Grand Masters of chess are thinking 10 to 15 moves ahead. The skillful project manager is much more akin to the Grand Master than to the average chess player. The skillful project manager is looking ahead to see what risks to the success of the project are lurking out there which are not clearly evident.

Risks are things which might happen. Issues are risks that are made reality. Unforeseen issues are the children of unforeseen risks. Most unforeseen risks are unforeseen because they defy assumptions made both during the formation of the project and while it evolves.

Every assumption is a risk. The skillful pm understands this and is constantly ferreting out and documenting assumptions. And along with each assumption documented, comes all the other activities I mention later on when documenting, analyzing, monitoring and managing risks.

Managing risks takes a very different form than managing issues.

Risks cannot be eliminated. There are only three strategies for handling risks:

1. Mitigation – reduce the probability and severity of the risk.
2. Transferal – make it someone else's problem. This is the whole idea behind the insurance industry.
3. Acceptance – some risks aren't worth the costs of mitigation or transferal. You are better off to simply accept the risk and set aside reserves to pay the costs if/when the risk becomes an issue.

Risks must be recognized, analyzed and managed proactively, reactively, or both.

The skillful PM always manages risks proactively, identifying and assessing them upfront and then making appropriate plans to mitigate, transfer, accept and monitor risks on an ongoing basis throughout the life of the project.

Not all the risks managed by the skillful PM appear on the publicized list of project risks. In fact, some of the most crucial risks, and their management is never noted on any report or found in any email.

These "undocumented" risks are those which are most politically sensitive and charged. They include risks like, "loss of executive support for this project," and "political infighting undermining the project," to name just a couple of these unmentionable risks.

I worked a project that would have saved a bank tens of millions of dollars every year, money that would have gone directly to the bottom-line and shareholder pockets. However, the project failed because I failed to be effective in managing the risks that arose from having two division heads who hated one another and needed to cooperate for the project to succeed.

Every other aspect of the project was well in hand. All the financial analyses were thoroughly vetted, the systems and processes analyzed. There was no question in the mind of anyone on the project that the end result would be a "home-run."

What none of us could imagine and manage was the fact that these two leaders hated each other so much, that they would rather see the project fail than to have the other get credit for any portion at all of the project success.

Foreseeing and successfully managing risks like these is not something that will typically be discussed in any project meeting, nor acknowledged in any written communication. However, if you fail to uncover and actively manage them, then you will fail.

In this case, the risk of the two managers not cooperating appeared to have been mitigated by the their own self-interests in delivering a win for the corporation. However, none of us involved foresaw that the depth of their animosity was sufficient to lead both of them to kill the effort rather than giving the other any credit at all.

The skillful PM is well versed in the myriad of different sorts of risks that can derail projects, especially those that will never be spoken of in public or private. S/he identifies all the risks, notes them, assesses the probabilities and impacts of each and prepares contingency plans for every significant risk. Some of those contingencies will be built into the project plans for all to see and understand. Others will only appear in your personal journal.

Along with each risk, the skillful PM will note what key indicators will let you know that the risk (possibility) is becoming a reality (issue). The skillful PM puts in place risk monitoring to provide the alert that things are not going as desired.

Because of this careful management and monitoring of risks, the skillful PM is rarely surprised by issues. Instead, the PM's monitoring shows that key indicators are heading the wrong direction long before the problem is evident to anyone else. With this kind of monitoring, the skillful PM seems to be almost psychic in their ability to head off problems almost before they become visible to anyone else.

Monitoring and contingency plans notwithstanding, stuff happens and issues will appear.

When a competent project manager takes over a project, a risk assessment is a standard exercise. Any reasonably competent project manager can sit down and list at least a half dozen or more risks which threaten every project. For the merely competent project manager, that assessment of the standard risks is enough. However, the skillful PM is looking much deeper and further into the organization and its context to uncover and prepare for the hidden risks.

Elsewhere in this book I discuss using conflict to your advantage. In that section I describe a simple exercise which, as a side effect of the conflict, brings to the immediate attention of the skillful PM risks that are usually hidden, unless you are already a subject matter expert in both the company and the field of achievement for the project. This exercise allows the existing subject matter experts to deliver to your feet the biggest risks, both obvious and hidden which threaten the success of the project. Although total reliance on the exercise I describe is inadvisable because there are often also large risks to which the denizens of a specific company may be blinded to by the corporate culture.

The skillful PM has internalized the processes of strategic planning and, on their own, craft a pretty decent SWOT (Strengths, Weaknesses, Opportunities and Threats) analysis which will identify both internal and external threats to the success of the project.

The skillful PM knows better than to rely solely upon her own inputs in a robust SWOT assessment. S/he knows how to ask pertinent questions of other knowledgeable stakeholders to validate SWOT assumptions and to uncover additional data to support a robust assessment of the risks.

Once the risks have been identified and validated with the project team and sponsors, the skillful PM knows how to quickly and painlessly augment the risk identification with an assessment that can be used to identify the appropriate risk management strategy (mitigate, transfer, or accept) and build preventative and countermeasures into the project plan which will enable early identification as risks emerge to become issues, and allow for rapid and decisive actions to resolve the root causes of those issues in ways that protect the success of the project and, by extension, the investment the client has made in the project.

While risks are managed (because they never go away), issues are resolved. Issues are always managed reactively, even if they were anticipated. For anticipated risks, contingency plans which reduce, transfer or move to accept the associated risk can be activated. For unanticipated issues, the first countermeasure is to determine the root cause of the issue (the unrecognized risk), and then decide on the appropriate risk management approach (mitigate, transfer, or accept).

Once an issue is identified and the root cause understood, the skillful PM knows to quantify the issue and develop the business case that will determine which approach to resolving the issue will be most likely to succeed and within acceptable limits for costs versus the benefits. Since, much of issue resolution is science more than art, I will leave off here on the science part.

Where art meets issue resolution is understanding which types of issues will be most unacceptable to the organization and making sure that you have given plenty of advance warning to the right people when you foresee such issues arising.

The Art of Project Management

© 2017 by alexmillos, Image used with permission through DepositPhotos.com

## CHAPTER 5: EFFECTIVE PROJECT FAILURE

> "Failure is an opportunity to begin again, more intelligently."
>
> Henry Ford

Any project manager who denies that s/he has had failures is either a liar or extremely new to the profession. Skillful project managers often have one or more spectacular failures in their portfolio. A project manager who has failed is not someone to be avoided. Failed projects are an inevitability.

For the skillful project manager the important things about failed projects are the lessons learned. The project manager to be avoided is the one who claims to have never failed, or who, when asked about the lessons learned from their failure consistently, even if subtly, ascribe their failures to the fault of someone else.

Learning from failure is essential to sustainable success.

Sometimes those lessons from failure are about the foundations of the project being built on sand, bad assumptions or a faulty understanding of the problem that was to be solved. Other failed projects are the results of the failure to foresee forces and events that destroyed the project team or the value proposition of the project. The reasons for failure are greater in number than there are projects in the world. Regardless, the skillful PM recognizes that failure to see these problems and navigate through them is the true failure of the project manager.

The skillful project manager learns from the reasons of these failures. Every failure teaches you pitfalls that you can avoid in another engagement.

This is especially true when the failure is something you should have been able to prevent.

- Was the unforeseen event or force something that you should have been aware of? How can you make sure you foresee these kinds of things the next time around?
- Was the failure the result of your inability to get team members to become an high-performing team? What can you do to get better at team building?

These are just a couple of the questions the skillful project manager asks whenever a project fails. And also when it succeeds.

Along with examining the root causes of project failure, the skillful project manager critically observes what went well. This examination should focus both on reinforcing what is working and on looking to see if there are ways to take what works and make it better, as well as on what is not working.

Failure to learn from failure is the only true failure. And, it is the unpardonable sin for a project manager.

A survey of articles on the most common causes of project failure yields some interesting patterns and at least one fact that should alarm every business that is planning on embarking on any large project.

The fact is this, that more than 50% of all large technology projects end in failure. This massive dissipation of shareholder value should result in top business executives and PMs specializing in managing large projects investing serious effort understanding why large projects fail and how to prevent that from happening.

An informal survey of articles on this topic revealed a pattern of failures which, I believe, the skillful PM can counter by appropriately applying both the arts and the sciences of project management.

At the top of the hit parade for project failure is a poorly defined project. When stated in that way, anyone will respond by saying, "Oh yes. Projects should be clearly defined."

In contrast, the skillful project manager asks the impertinent question, "what is the problem you are trying to solve with this project?" Followed closely behind with "why do you think this project will solve that problem?"

All too often, when the PM attempts to ask these questions, the response from corporate management is to pat the PM on the head (metaphorically) and say, "Smarter heads than yours figured out the need for this project. Yours is not to reason why. Yours is but to do, or die."

**"Into the valley of death rode the six-hundred…"**
Alfred, Lord Tennyson
The Charge of the Light Brigade

The skillful pm will not be deterred by such management disdain or sleight of hand, but will either insist on a root cause analysis, or will walk away rather than foolishly taking on a project where the foundational reasons are neither fully understood nor plainly articulated.

The second biggest reason listed for large project failures is inadequate risk management. This takes as many varied forms as there are types of risks. This includes inadequate risk analysis, communications failures, lack of appropriate and effective tracking and measurement, lack of formal methods and strategies, lack of documentation, lack of appropriately detailed project plans, inadequate requirements, etc.

As I mentioned above, project management is, at its core, risk management.

The third most common cause of large project failure, and the one I believe is the root cause of the two previous causes, is inadequately skilled project managers.

Often this failure is listed as inadequate training, but training alone is insufficient to create a skillful project manager. Experience is the key crucible for shaping a properly trained project manager and turning him or her into a truly skillful project manager.

When I hire project managers onto large projects, I never hire based on potential (theoretical) performance. I always insist on proven performance, delivering the same kind of large projects.

The only place I hire for potential, is when I am hiring someone who will be working for a proven and experienced PM. And then, only if the budget and timelines of the project allow for the luxury of extended learning curves.

When a client hires a PM who has proven experience delivering projects of the same type, size and scale (or bigger), they get project managers who quickly begin to deliver significant results and who have very short learning curves. But, that kind of proven experience doesn't come cheap.

When a client balks at paying the rates charged by top-shelf, skillful project managers who have proven experience with large projects, they had better add a lot of money to the budget and time to the schedule to pay for the learning curve that the entire company will be going through at the hands of what the articles on the causes of project failure call "inadequately trained project managers."

It is my hope that both top business managers and project managers will read this book and be able to more accurately assess the gap between what they need and what they have in both the art and science of project management, they will recognize the difference between the two, and this book will help them see how to close the gaps in the art of project management.

## CHAPTER 6: ASK THE RIGHT QUESTIONS

*"In school, we're rewarded for having the answer, not for asking a good question."*
Richard Saul Wurman

Asking good questions is a hallmark of successful analysts. They know what questions to ask so that they can unearth the core of a system requirement or a problem. Likewise, the skillful project manager knows how to ask good questions.

Although many project managers are brought on board once the project has been funded, the skillful project manager will still swim upstream and ask questions that will reveal the root causes of the problem the project is expected to resolve.

Asking these questions can seem impertinent or a waste of time to many. However, if you deliver the project on-time and within-budget, but it doesn't deliver the business results, it won't be considered a success. If the project is attacking the symptoms instead of the root causes of a problem, it will never deliver the desired business results.

While to some it appears suicidal or stupid to question the root causes and problem statement for a project, both personal integrity and good business sense requires that the skillful project manager dance in this particular minefield until the root causes are truly understood and you can confirm that the successfully executed project will resolve those root causes in whole or in part.

While running a program management office (PMO) one of my project managers came to me near review time, deeply concerned about her upcoming performance review.

"Why are you worried," I asked her.

"Because I have killed every project you assigned me to manage this year," she confessed.

"Well, let's look at what you have done." We then proceeded to examine each project she had "killed." I noted how much the project budget was and then asked why she killed the project. In every case her response was the same.

"After I got into the project, I realized that they were treating a symptom, not the root cause and the project would not deliver the expected results to the business."

"So, by killing all these projects you prevented the company from wasting all these millions of dollars in budgeted funds on projects that would have failed to pay back the investment?" I concluded.

"I guess so," she admitted.

"I think your performance review will come out just fine," I told her. And it did.

The skillful project manager can often add more value to an engagement by questioning and uncovering root causes than by blindly accepting funding and project scope statements and charging forward to deliver tasks on time and within budget. Questioning the foundation of the project may be uncomfortable for everyone involved, but it is essential for success.

Asking those questions in ways that don't embarrass or alienate the project sponsors requires the ability to be tactful, diplomatic, and non-threatening while driving to the heart of the matter and uncovering any false assumptions that may undergird and ultimately sabotage your project.

If you don't already know how to conduct a root cause analysis, using tools like an Ishikawa (fish bone) Diagram, then you need to take time to learn, or find someone who you can bring in on projects to expertly fulfill this need on a contract basis. I learned how to do this in the world of Total Quality Management. Today, Six Sigma lessons are the most common place to learn these tools. The ability to rapidly and correctly uncover root causes is a very valuable and somewhat rare skill.

Using the Ishikawa diagram is part of the science of project management. Knowing when to use it, and getting your management team to participate is a root cause analysis is within the art of project management.

Often, the most valuable (and annoying) question you can ask is "Why?" And, like the six-year-old child who continues to ask it, you too must ask it again and again.

This simple, but effective question, if asked enough, almost always results in greater understanding of why the project exists, why people oppose or favor it, why someone is trying to manipulate you into doing something for them., or why they are following the processes they currently embrace.

Here is a quick example:

"Why are you doing things this way?"
"Because that is our process or procedure?"
"Why is this your procedure?"
"Because we had this problem some years ago and this solution was implemented."
"Why are you still doing it this way?"
"I don't know. That problem doesn't exist anymore."

BINGO! Now, you can either eliminate wasted effort, of find out if the process solves some other problem.

Being able to ask good questions, without putting people on the defensive, angering them, or, making them feel you are wasting their time requires that you build both rapport and confidence with them before you start down this road.

One other key aspect to good questions is that they are

typically open-ended. Let's take the example above and recast it with closed-ended questions so you can see how useless they are.

"Why are you doing things this way?"
"Because that is our process or procedure?"
"Do you know why this is your procedure?"
"Yes."
"Do you know why are you still doing it this way?"
"No."

You are now at a dead-end. Instead of finding a lever to change things for the better, this line of questions has made the person answering feel ignorant and probably defensive and you have no idea of what the original problem was and if it still exists.

Consistently asking open-ended questions requires thought. Keeping the subject talking requires good conversation skills and may include taking some notes, or using other methods to let the speaker know you are finding their information valuable.

Elsewhere in this book I point out that the skillful PM uses good questions to help determine if business requirements are robust and verifiable. I point out that the reactions of the business experts to your questions is often a better indicator than the actual text of the document.

Asking a business expert, "what would it take to make your business requirements complete and clear enough that they could serve as the basis for a training manual for someone to your job," may get a laugh or a snarl. Regardless, the skillful PM will correctly read if the reaction is hiding something or not.

Being a thoughtful inquisitor and a good conversationalist are not matters of science, numbers and calculations. They are matters of art, requiring you to be self-aware, aware of others and aware of what their body language, tonality, and words are telling you while you are talking with them.

> "He who asks a question is a fool for five minutes; he who does not ask a question remains a fool forever."
>
> Chinese proverb

© Copyright 2017 by @ Boris15 , Image used with permission through DepositPhotos.com

## CHAPTER 7: THE IMPACTS OF CHANGE

"Change is inevitable.  Improvement is optional."
John C Maxwell

In my office hangs a poster.  It looks like one of those wonderful, glossy motivational posters we have all seen.  It is actually created by the company Despair.com.  The picture is of a tornado.  In large letters below the image is says, "Change."  Below that in smaller letters, it reads, "when the winds of change blow hard enough, even the smallest item can become a deadly projectile."

Although the folks at Despair.com call this poster a "demotivational" poster, in this case I disagree.  For me, this poster is an admonition to project managers.  It warns them to pay attention to the details.  Failure to pay attention to seemingly inconsequential details can often have devastating impacts on a project. Project management is all about change.  Every project is a change to the status quo.

The successful implementation of a project will change how or what the organization is doing, or both.  And change is stressful, individually and collectively.

The skillful PM realizes that s/he is a change agent and is not blind to this significant source of conflict and stress that focuses on both the project and the PM.

While conflict and stress can be managed to help produce superior results (see the respective chapters elsewhere in this book), that is only possible if the PM is aware of the potential for stress and conflict and is prepared to skillfully use those powerful forces to move forward toward the desired results of the project.

Ignoring the effects of change is as dangerous as ignoring any other project-threatening risk. Change management is an essential skill of the effective project manager. And, an essential component of change management is communication.

Never forget that change is as stressful and traumatic for the proponents of the change as it is for the opponents. Just because a key executive is a project sponsor doesn't mean that s/he is an unflinching advocate for and defender of the change. If you don't manage the change-induced stresses of your supporters as well as that of your opponents, you can expect to find "arrows" in your back from those you thought were backing you up as you moved the project forward into the face of opposition.

A combat veteran I know once explained "friendly fire" to me. He said that the first time you get into a fire fight with the enemy, the bullets start flying, scores get settled with people getting shot or killed, and then you start shooting at the enemy. That may be a very unflattering picture of combat, but it is very illustrative of what can happen even within a project team when the change you are engineering meets with organizational resistance or even outright opposition.

For the skillful project manager, managing change is about turning resistance into active cooperation. That is neither easy nor simple. It requires the realization that resistance is not entirely a bad thing. Deftly handled, it can enable you to produce a better result than if you tried to ignore or steam roller over it (see conflict management elsewhere in this book). Seeking out resistance, perhaps even voicing some yourself can be exactly what is needed to allow you to uncover and resolve the root causes of risks that would otherwise rise up at the last moment and destroy the value of your work.

Before you can effectively manage a change, you need to be able to clearly articulate not only what will be the end result of the change, but what benefits will come from the change and what problems will be removed by the change. If you don't know or are not able to clearly articulate these points, then your efforts to change the organization are unlikely to succeed.

Once you know these answers and can articulate them clearly, you will need to understand the avenues of communication in the organization, both formal and informal, and then define a plan to use those channels to communicate your messages to all the stakeholders as you need and want.

The purposes of your communication plan are to increase the comfort level of the individuals that comprise and contribute to the success of your project and to incrementally win them over to support your efforts. You will do that by skillfully communicating the messages I mentioned above, along with providing them information on the progress of your efforts.

As noted elsewhere, the skillful project manager is possessed of a great degree of self-knowledge. If your communications skills are not superlative, then you should bring on communications specialists to craft your messages to have the desired effects. Having someone dedicated to managing your communications activities is very helpful and totally required when you are driving a large, high-profile, high-risk project.

The communications professional will keep your communications plan on track and will go a long way towards building and sustaining the support you need to succeed.

If you don't have a communications specialist to augment your own skills and efforts, then you will just have to pay the price yourself to keep working the lines of communication effectively to achieve your objectives.

By allaying the concerns of your stakeholders through your communications efforts, you decrease their stress (and resistance) relative to the change you are implementing. Done correctly, you can not only eliminate resistance in many places, you can create demand for your change, along with the associated commitment to implement the change faithfully and fully.

Reducing the angst around the change allows your stakeholders to relegate your change efforts to a small corner of their daily concerns, allowing them to focus on their ordinary daily demands instead of being distracted from these key duties by concerns about what you are, or are not going to do to their work world.

The skillful PM also realizes that the change being promoted by this project may very well be one of many changes happening at the same time. Too much change at the same time will overload the very people you need to help you succeed.

Assessing the level of change in your target organization is essential to success. Despite the merits of your project, and your skill at communication them, too much change will distract and detract from what you are trying to accomplish.

If you cannot negotiate a reduction in the amount and timing of change, then you may need to walk away before the entire organization goes into reset-mode and rejects all changes, along with those who are driving them.

Fortunately, in recent years, many organizations have established risk management practices within their company and the knowledge of operational risk has come along with that skillset. The implementation risks associated with the size and scope of large projects are understood by operational risk professionals and they can often become your ally in helping the organization to reduce the risk of project failure by limiting the pace and scale of changes.

© 2017 by thinglass, used with permission through DepositPhotos.com

## CHAPTER 8: HIRING RIGHT

"I hire people brighter than me and I get out of their way."
Lee Iacocca

In the book *Built to Last*, authors Jim Collins and Jerry Porras use a metaphor about the people on your team. They note that it is fundamentally important to get the right people on the bus. After you get the right people on the bus, you need to get them in the right seat(s) to get your bus where you want it to be.

However, if you have the wrong people on the bus, it won't matter what seat you have them in, they still will never help you get the bus where you need it go.

Great coaches are careful recruiters. To build a great team, recruits need to be 'A' players who fit with your team's strategy and culture. If you want to build high performing teams, you need to be a careful recruiter, and a great coach.

Here are four key points I have identified that will help you to hire right.

## FOUR KEY POINTS FOR HIRING RIGHT

1. Don't just accept just anyone on your team. If you want a great team, this is one area you cannot afford to delegate. Do your own interviewing and hiring.

    Every year the professional basketball, football and baseball leagues hold a ritual called a draft, where they take turns picking who they want on their team for the next year. After the draft, it is not uncommon for teams to swap players or to trade draft picks before the actual event. In all cases this is because they want to get the right player(s) for their team.

    They engage in almost non-stop recruiting to consider players from all over. And colleges all across the U.S. are constantly scouting and recruiting players to make their athletic teams into high-performing teams that will bring prestige (and money) to their university.

    Often, as a PM you are given a team, without any opportunity for you to pick them. In these cases, I still interview every team member. I may, or may not, make it formal, but I ask pretty much all the same questions I would in a hiring interview. It allows me to gauge the person as well as to communicate my expectations to them. If I find they don't match, I register that as a risk with the project sponsor, which opens the door for subsequent conversations if the person proves to be an impediment rather than an asset.

2. Don't hire the best of the worst. Establish the standards for the role(s) you are filling and be prepared to start the recruiting process all over if none of your pool of candidates meets the standard. Hiring the best of the worst is just another way of hiring substandard employees. Substandard teammates will always cost more than it does to delay things until you have people who can do the work without you doing it for them.

3. Hire people smarter than you. If you feel the need to always be the smartest person in the room (or on your team), then be prepared to live a life awash in mediocrity. When you build a team of people who are smarter than you, not only does it make you look smarter, it pushes you to up your own game. Chess players know that getting better requires playing against people who play better than you.

   Napoleon Hill, author of _Think and Grow Rich_, when writing about how the richest industrialists of his day built their businesses, coined the phrase, "Mastermind Group." Each of these men built a team of people who were each smarter in their own field that Henry Ford, Andrew Carnegie, or John Rockefeller were. These men became giants of industry because they hired and retained people smarter than themselves. Their respective mastermind groups were integral to their phenomenal success. Your project team needs to be your Mastermind Group.

4. Hire those who can deliver today, and tomorrow. Hire people with proven track records delivering the skills and work that you need right now. And, who have the ability to grow and learn so that they can increase and improve their abilities as the needs of your team change over time and people have to take on new or additional roles.

   When I hire, I don't hire for potential performance. I hire for proven performance at the level I need, and with the potential to deliver more.

Experienced managers know that attitude is often more important than experience. But, the two cannot be mutually exclusive. If you don't have the luxury of being able to train someone into their role, then you need to hire for both attitude and experience. If you cannot find a candidate with both, then keep looking.

As a project manager, you may or may not have the opportunity to formally hire your team members. Even if you can hire some, it is pretty certain that many of your team members will be forced into your team because of their existing roles or expertise in your client's company.

Even if you must accept someone onto your team without your consent, the skillful PM will find ways to "interview" these members of the team and determine if their attitude and experience can be turned to the advantage of the project. Doing this, you may also uncover shortcomings of knowledge or experience which you can find other ways to fill and which might otherwise have hurt your efforts before you realized there was a gap between what you need in the team and what the team is able to deliver.

The skillful PM knows how to conduct effective interviews to determine if you have the right people and if they are in the right seat (role).

Rather than belabor here all the ins-and-outs of effective interviews I will refer you to my book on the topic, "*Tips for Effective Interviews*." In that volume you will learn the basics of the most effective interview techniques I know for uncovering both attitudes and experience.

Since that book is primarily aimed at job seekers there are some points that I need to make here, beyond what are mentioned in that volume.

The skillful PM knows enough about organizational design and development, as well as the processes of project management (not to mention self-awareness) to figure out the roles needed to successfully deliver a given project as well as the experience, knowledge and attitudes needed to work with you to make that happen.

In this space, science must precede and act as the foundation for the art of project management, so I will give you a bit of the science to lead you to the art.

For each role needed to successfully deliver a project, the skillful PM will identify the concomitant knowledge, experience, and attitude(s) needed to succeed in that role.

Having identified these factors, you need to weight them in importance for success. The weighting may be influenced by compensating factors in the organization or project such as training budgets, timelines, and supplement staff.

Having identified and weighted each factor you must now get to the hardest part of the interview process, i.e, crafting questions that will allow your candidates to reveal themselves.

For each attitude, knowledge, and type/level of experience you seek, you should craft no less than three questions. And the questions need to be built the right way.

Every question should begin with the phrase, "Tell me about a time when…" This will help you to determine if the candidate has actual experience or is just providing you with an hypothetical (textbook) answer. The only exception to this should be when you have determined that a hypothetical response will help to reveal their actual thought processes – such as asking them to solve a problem.

I will give a disclaimer here that no interview technique is fool proof. I have had instances where both the résumé and interview made me believe I had a competent, experienced candidate. However, once they got into the role and couldn't perform, it became obvious that they had simply gamed the system. Unfortunately, that meant they got promptly fired for poor performance, an experience that was almost as painful for me as I am sure it was for them.

Still, I will say that this behavioral interviewing technique, known as the STAR method is more effective and reliable than any other interview technique that I know.

It is referred to as the STAR technique because when the candidate is answering your questions, you are looking for them to describe their actual situation or task (ST), their own personal activities (A), and the results (R) of their actions.

One of the biggest challenges I have found in using this technique is getting candidates to stop using team-speak, talking about what "we" did and cite their own, individual actions.

After the second time of reminding or correcting them to talk about their own actions instead of saying "we", I generally disqualify the candidate because it shows they aren't good communicators, they cannot take directions well, and they are slow learners. Any one of those three is enough to disqualify a candidate from the high-performing teams I assemble to successfully execute my clients' high-risk, high-profile projects.

I don't claim to own the STAR method. It is a technique I was taught when I was required to interview hundreds of candidates for a variety of roles. I have successfully used it and taught it to both managers and job seekers all over the country.

All this talk about interviewing skills is all about getting the right people on the bus. When some team members are forced on you, the right person to get on the bus may be someone who can make up for the deficiencies or baggage that one of your "forced hires" may bring along. But, until you have gotten to know the team members you inherited, you won't know who else you need on the bus with you.

If you have the right people on the bus, and get them into the right seat, the next bit of work, motivating them, is immensely easier.

© 2017 by @ iqoncept, used with permission through DepositPhotos.com

## CHAPTER 9: MOTIVATING OTHERS

"Do unto others, what they want to have done unto them."
                                        Tom Sheppard

The skillful PM understands the rules of motivation and applies them deftly.  This knowledge stems from an understanding of motivation as described by the likes of <u>Abraham Maslow's hierarchy of needs</u>, <u>Frederick Herzberg's hygiene factors</u> and  a bit of applied psychology.

Once you move your team members beyond the foundations of <u>Maslow's hierarchy of needs</u> and into the realms of <u>Herzberg's Hygiene Factors</u>, you must come to two, conflicting realizations:

1) All human beings roughly share the same motivational imperatives.
2) Each human being places different value on each motivational imperative based on their
    a. Experience
    b. Lifecycle stage
    c. Current circumstances

What this means for the skillful PM is that while you can use general motivational methods for many people, when you are faced with the need to motivate a particular individual, you must find out what that individual values most and find ways to use that knowledge to entice their compliance with your will. The most skillful PM will achieve that motivation without being obviously overt.

The capstone of motivation stems from a correct understanding of what is often referred to in Christianity as "the Golden Rule."

The Golden Rule is generally stated as treating others as you would like to be treated.

Unfortunately, this statement too often leads to a profound misunderstanding and anything but golden results. A restatement of the Golden Rule may lead to greater clarity and proper application.

I suggest the Golden Rule be restated to say, you should treat others the way they want to be treated.

The crux of this restatement is that you want to be treated the way you want to be treated. Someone else wants to be treated the way they want to be treated. And the way they want to be treated may be very different than the way you want to be treated.

As an example, I am a very straightforward individual. I am not easily offended and I don't wed my ego to my ideas. When I present ideas, if you disagree with me on some point, I would rather you say so and let's discuss it. If that discussion happens in a meeting with others present, usually I am fine with that. The public discussion usually invites additional input and can ultimately result in a much better outcome than would have been produced by simply applying my original notions.

Other managers feel humiliated, offended, and personally

attacked if someone publicly disagrees with them. In a private setting, they may be perfectly reasonable and open to discussion. But, when confronted in a public setting, they entrench themselves in their position, resist change, and are not amenable to seeing a different viewpoint.

Which behavior is wrong?

Neither.

My way of handling disagreement versus that of another is neither right nor wrong, they are simply different. I like my own approach because it tends to be effective and efficient. However, if my approach results in ill will, resentment, and passive-aggression, then it is neither effective nor efficient. So, the right way, depends on the players involved. The right way is to treat others the way they want to be treated, not the way you want to be treated.

Napoleon Hill is probably best known for his book <u>*Think and Grow Rich*</u>. A lesser-known work, that I have found to be essential is his <u>*Law of Success in Sixteen Lessons.*</u> Lesson 16 is on the Golden Rule. Hill professes that the Golden Rule is based upon a natural law often referred to as the Law of the Harvest. You reap what you sow. Or, in other words, you get what you give.

If you give disrespect, dishonesty, disloyalty, anger, discourtesy and arrogance, that is what will come back at you, sooner or later. Conversely, if you give respect, honesty, loyalty, patience, courtesy and humility that is what you will harvest in the treatment of others toward you.

**A word about fairness.** Fairness is a much-praised virtue in leaders. It is also probably the most totally misunderstood and misrepresented notion.

Most people, when they talk about fairness are actually asking for an equality of outcomes. They want the same pay for the same job, regardless of how well they are doing the job compared to others in the same role. In fact, most folks who cry loudest for fairness would actually run screaming from the room if they were treated fairly. It would mean that they got punished for every infraction and all punishments would be equal, not adjusted or mitigated by circumstances.

True fairness is about rewarding or punishing people according to their own merits and in ways that will have the most desirable effect upon them.

Treating everyone equally is the pinnacle of unfairness. Treating people with fairness, while allowing for some weakness or failure, still rewards people according to their level of contribution.

Treating everyone equally is a disincentive for excellent or extraordinary contribution. If the slacker is given the same praise as the miracle-worker, human nature being what it is, the miracle worker will soon desist, while the slacker will continue. In the end, you will be able to treat everyone equally, because everyone will be slackers together, doing the absolute minimum amount needed to get by. This approach will absolutely create an environment where *Theory X* management, the slave-master mentality, will necessarily prevail.

It would it lead to the slave-master mentality because, when people are denied the increased rewards that should accrue as a result of increased labor, then they are effectively enslaved, and the slave mentality will begin to consume them and lower their efforts to align with the minimum they must do in order to avoid punishment while receiving the minimal reward which is provided for all labor, great or small.

The reward for the slave is, at best, subsistence. It is food, shelter, and clothing, but none of these in abundance.

In contrast with the slavery ensuing from an equality doctrine, a fairness doctrine provides greater rewards for greater results.

The worker who produces more, earns more. The entrepreneur who delivers more value to others, earns more. And both enjoy the fruits of their labors without fear of confiscation for some "greater good." Although, they are both free to share their abundance to whatever degree and with whomever, they see fit.

> **"Treating everyone equally means … deploying another power strategy, redistributing people's rewards in a way that they determine."**
>
> *The 48 Laws of Power*

The Art of Project Management

© Copyright 2017 by @ RomanPashkovsky, Image used with permission through DepositPhotos.com

## CHAPTER 10: FIVE RULES OF COMMUNICATIONS

"The art of communication is the language of leadership."
James Humes

A reader of mine recently suggested I do a piece on communications and some proven rules for successful communication, particularly with regards to emails and text messages. Given this focus on the perils of written communications I wanted to start from some well-known "facts" about written communications.

    **FACT:** Communication requires three basic elements: a sender, a receiver, and a medium. In our world today, a very large portion of our communications with others rely wholly upon the written medium. The biggest problem with written communications is that it relies wholly upon the smallest portion of what people use to understand messages, words.

    **MYTH:** Like me, many of you have probably heard that only a small percentage of our meaning is derived from the actual words of our communications, with the remainder being conveyed by our tone of voice (tonality) and our body language. I wanted to get the percentages right, so I went looking for the numbers and their source.

I quickly found many articles presenting a 7-18-55 formula for communications where 7 means that 7% of the meaning is based on words, 18% is conveyed by tonality and 55% is based on body language (including facial expressions). The source cited for this proportion is the Mehrabian studies on communications. This is a reference to a couple of studies conducted in 1967 by Dr. Albert Mehrabian which he published in a book called <u>Silent Messages: Implicit Communication of Emotions and Attitudes</u>.

Unfortunately, Dr. Mehrabian (and a few others) have been valiantly trying to point out that his study doesn't say what people think it says. You begin to get an inkling of this from the subtitle of the book, "Implicit Communication of <u>Emotions</u> and <u>Attitudes</u>" [my emphasis]. His much touted numbers of 7-18-55 were, in reality, focusing on the weight we give to each of those factors when the explicit attitudinal or emotional message of the words seems to conflict with the implicit attitudinal or emotional message of the tone or body language or both.

To restate this a bit more clearly, when someone you care about says, "I'm fine," you take note of the tone of voice, and then the body language that accompanies those words to see if they are all consistent and this person you care about is truly "fine" or not. When the other two signals agree with the words, you believe what is said. When the words don't agree with the tone or body language or both, you don't believe the words.

Mehrabian has been careful to clarify that all he was talking about is when the three elements of communication are in some degree of conflict. So, it is not true to state that 7% of the meaning in our communications is embodied in the words we use.

**The After Myth**

Having cut us adrift from the safety of the 7-18-55 formula, how then can we consider the effectiveness of our communications? Unfortunately, It has been my experience that any writing which can be emotionally or attitudinally misinterpreted, will be. Because of this propensity for misinterpretation, written communications should be handled with at least as much care as you would when laying hands on a venomous snake.

## Rule #1 – Judicious Use of Emotion Words

First off, although the 7-18-55 formula is not the firm mathematical model we may have believed it to be, it does tell us something useful. It lets us know that listeners apply different factors when they consider the meaning of communications received. In the absence of tone and body language, the recipient is left to their own devices to guess at what tone and attitude is coming along with the written word. Receivers are likely to "hear" the tone of your message and "see" your expressions using their own filter for your messages, instead of your filter. This is a communication (and relationship) minefield. Their filter can be twisted by not only your relationship but by their own state of mind at the time of receipt.

Some writers a quick to note the value of adding emoticons to your emails and instant messages. While it is true that emoticons are helpful, they are not absolutely reliable for conveying your true tone.

As I considered the difficulty of accurately conveying your tone in writing, I pondered how great authors have managed to clearly convey their attitude and emotions while solely using the written word (especially in the days before the rubber-crutch of emoticons). What I discovered is that the great communicators of the past, expressly conveyed their attitudes with words that described their feelings. Consider the lack of ambiguity in the following phrases:

"It is with deepest regret that I…"
"I was delighted when I read about your…"
"I wanted to curl up under my desk in a fetal position when…"
"I was disappointed when…"
"I was annoyed when…"
"I was confused when…"
"I felt defensive when…"

Are you seeing a theme here? We are trained to make our

business writing devoid of emotion. Many of us are very adept at it. However, if you want to influence the emotional filter others use when they are trying to understand your message, then you need to be explicit in expressing your own emotion. Here is a more concrete example which we can spin several different ways.

A. "In our staff meeting this afternoon, when you mentioned the accomplishments of me and my team, I was surprised that you took it on yourself instead of letting me present this to the group."

B. "In our staff meeting this afternoon, when you mentioned the accomplishments of me and my team, I was surprised and upset that you took it on yourself instead of letting me present this to the group."

C. "In our staff meeting this afternoon, when you mentioned the accomplishments of me and my team, I was surprised and delighted that you took it on yourself instead of letting me present this to the group."

In all three examples, I express that I was surprised. But, with "A" it is not entirely clear if I was pleasantly surprised, or not. In "B" and "C", I add one emotional word and my emotional tone becomes clear. In "B" I am definitely not happy. In "C" I am definitely happy. With a minor change, I have removed the ambiguity.

The problem with "A" above, is that my reader is left to his or her own imaginings when reading my note. If I have difficult relationship with the reader, chances are good that person will believe I am not happy. If my relationship with the reader is good, that person will likely assume I am happy with what was done. In either case, the recipient has only a 50/50 chance of getting it right, unless you add explicitly emotional language to clarify.

Don't get me wrong here. I am not advocating that you add emotional language to all your emails. In fact, in most business communications you want to stick to the facts when writing and wait for a face-to-face situation to allow your feelings on the topic to show at all. Emotional language carries its own risks. If you don't choose your words carefully enough, or you use it too much, you may convey an image of emotional volatility. Go back and read "B" above and consider the word "upset." Upset is a bit ambiguous. It clearly conveys displeasure, but the degree of upset is subject to interpretation by the reader. I can either add a modifier, e.g., very, mildly, extremely, etc., or, I can replace it with a more accurate word, e.g., disappointed, angry, enraged, annoyed, etc.

The most ambiguous (ambiguous = dangerous) form of communication is sarcasm. With sarcasm, the tone, body language and words may all be approximately aligned to convey a message which is the exact opposite of the intent of the communication. Humorous sarcasm reduces significant amounts of ambiguity by deliberately making both the tone and body language at odds with the words themselves. Mean sarcasm deliberately reduces the discontinuity of words, tone and body language so that the recipient may be further humiliated by believing the words of the message instead of their opposite.

When it comes to the written word, sarcasm is almost impossible to consistently and accurately communicate. I have seen many (too many) emails where the sender was attempting to use humorous sarcasm and was instead taken at their word, causing a great deal of confusion, and too often inspiring hard feelings when none were intended. When it comes to writing, my rule for sarcasm is, just say, "no."

If you attempt it, be prepared for problems. If you try to call it out when you use it by writing, "I mean that sarcastically," you lose the effect you wanted and risk having people read more than you intended as sarcasm. Just say, "no."

While writing this piece, I was put in mind of the fictional story of _Anne Shirley_. If you have never read or seen this story its namesake character is delightful in her use of extremely emotional language to remove any ambiguity in her communications, in the extreme. Some of her most notable phrases are:

"This is a wound I shall bear forever."
"My life is a perfect graveyard of buried hopes."
"Red hair is my life-long sorrow."
"I am in the depths of despair."
"I am well in body although considerably rumpled up in spirit…"

"I love Diana so, Marilla. I cannot ever live without her."
"I hate him furiously."
"How sadly things have changed…"
"… it makes SUCH a difference. It LOOKS so much nicer."

These quotes show a rich use of language which convey a breadth and depth of emotion which is almost breathtaking.

## Rule #2 – Use the Attributes of the Written Word to Your Advantage

The last Anne Shirley quote noted above uses attributes of the written word to convey an emphasis which is otherwise absent. Take note and learn to use ALL CAPS, *italics*, <u>underline</u>, and **bold** to allow you to emphasize what <u>you</u> want.

ALL CAPS for emails is generally considered to be SHOUTING, or at least raising your voice. Use it very sparingly as a tool for emphasis. Consider how our examples from above take on additional emphasis with the use of capital letters.

A. "In our staff meeting this afternoon, when YOU mentioned the accomplishments of me and my team, I was surprised that you took it on yourself instead of letting me present this to the group."
B. "In our staff meeting this afternoon, when YOU mentioned the accomplishments of me and my team, I was surprised and UPSET that you took it on yourself instead of letting me present this to the group."
C. "In our staff meeting this afternoon, when YOU mentioned the accomplishments of me and my team, I was surprised and DELIGHTED that you took it on yourself instead of letting me present this to the group."

You should be able to readily discern from this example how adding capitals increases the perceived degree of emotion expressed and emphasized that is was "YOU" instead of someone else who mentioned these accomplishments.

## Rule #3 – The Rule of 3

A sure sign that emotions are escalating, regardless of the

verbiage involved, is when the number of emails on a topic is rapidly increasing or the number of people copied on the message is increasing, or both. Another sign is when the explicitly emotional words in the message chain are piling up.

My reader, who challenged me to write this post, noted that she has a rule of 3. If an email exchange has gone through three cycles (message and reply is one cycle) and the issue is still not resolved, it is time to pick up the phone or walk down the hall for a one-on-one with the other party.

When you pick up the phone, you can control the tone of your voice instead of having the reader "hear" you through his or her own filter. When you sit across the room from your message recipient, you can add your body language to your tone to reinforce the emotion or attitude you want to convey with your words. This significantly reduces the ambiguity and room for misinterpretation of your message.

**Rule #4 – Take a Breath**

A colleague of mine, when dealing with a difficult key player, ignored the Rule of 3 and lost her job over it.

A series of emails had gone back and forth between my colleague and another key player, often with seconds between responses. The list of people copied on the communications continued to grow and emotions were escalating rapidly as positions began to harden in the face of increased organizational visibility.

Our boss intervened and with a series of face-to-face meetings, phone calls and judicious emails she reduced the number of people on the email exchange back down to the necessary few, she had succeeded in dramatically reducing emotional tensions and was nearing successful closure on the issue.

At that critical moment, my colleague almost instantly responded to another, related, email from the other key player, copying again the many people who had previously been made privy to the discussion. The immediate and breathtakingly rapid effect was to fully re-ignite all the emotional drama and escalate it to a new level, completing undoing all the fragile fence-mending our boss had just achieved.

Before sunset, my colleague was out of a job.

This real-life story about the Rule of 3 also serves to highlight a general rule of communication, especially potentially contentious communication. When you get a message that stimulates a strong emotional response, don't respond immediately. If you respond immediately, you will likely have strong emotions shaping your response. Strong emotions generally cloud your thinking and don't allow you to carefully consider all relevant facts in the situation.

This notion of metaphorically or actually taking a deep breath and letting it out slowly while counting to ten, applies regardless of the communication medium. Think about that the next time you are on your favorite social media and see a post that evokes a strong emotional reaction. Look at the chain of comments below the post. Note the timestamps between the most vitriolic comments and replies.

Social media may display an exaggerated view of this principle in action (or being ignored), but an eerily similar scene can, and does, play out in businesses every day. As a professional, don't be guilty of the escalating emotional response. The price you will pay for hasty words can be extremely high.

## Rule #5 – What Gets Written Stays Written

One final point. You have likely heard the joke, "what happens in Vegas, stays in Vegas," and its internet counterpoint, "what happens on the internet, stays on the internet forever." When it comes to written communications remember the words of Job (Job 31) in *The Bible*, "that mine adversary had written a book. Surely I would take it upon my shoulder, and bind it as a crown to me... as a prince I would go near unto him."

The threat here is clear. When you put something in writing, it can be used against you. This is even true of instant messages. Screen captures are easy to do without your knowledge, and then your hasty words, written with a presumption of confidentiality, can be brought back to be used against you.

Having exploded the 7-18-55 myth of communications, I didn't want to leave you adrift, so I have given you five rules for written communications which have proven useful to me and

many other professionals. Use them well. Remember:
1. Judiciously use emotion words to establish the emotion you intend to convey.
2. Use the attributes of the written word to place emphasis where <u>you</u> want it.
3. Apply the "rule of 3" and change your communication medium from writing to verbal or face-to-face to short circuit a communication crisis.
4. Take a breath before responding.
5. What gets written stays written.

© 2017 by londondeposit, image used with permission through DepositPhotos.com

## CHAPTER 11: OFFICE POLITICS

**In war, you can only be killed once, but in politics, many times.**
Winston Churchill

Corporate politics are all about power. They are power games. Power games are always dangerous, and regardless of your opinion of them, they cannot be ignored. For a PM, power games are especially treacherous, because very often the PM has little or no inherent organizational power. As an example, hiring and firing decisions may be influenced by the PM, but are not usually decided by the PM. Even though a PM may have budgetary responsibility, rarely does the PM have the authority to decide how, when and what expenditures will be paid.

While all that may be true, a skillful PM will steadily bring power to bear where and when needed. Usually, it will be the power of others, but directed by the influence of the PM.

The ability to direct Other Peoples' Power (OPP) depends upon the PM's ability to influence others. And the ability to influence others depends upon the credibility and likability of the PM.

The skillful PM does not overtly play office politics, but s/he does know how to navigate them successfully.

The best course is to keep yourself above the fray of office politics. Be friendly to all sides and commit yourself to none of them. As soon as you commit to some office faction, your ability to deliver results is decreased. By making yourself a clear ally to some, you clearly make yourself an enemy to others. Those enemies may choose to play their games through either passive or aggressive resistance. In either case, you will likely find yourself deprived of key resources when you need them most.

Keeping above the fray is not possible if you are ignorant of and eschewing office politics. Keeping yourself above the fray is a much more difficult political ploy than you might imagine.

If you ignore the politics that swirl around you, you will fall victim to them. You will become a pawn in the games between different power players. The challenge, inherent in staying above the fray, is to be seen publicly as neutral toward all, and privately as friend to all. Your only true interest or alliance, your emotional commitment, must be to deliver the value of your project to the business. You must be committed to this end regardless of what its delivery means to the individuals impacted, and how much you may like or dislike them.

## Dissecting *The Black Book of Executive Politics*: A Detailed Book Review

The following review was originally published by me on my blog and on LinkedIn. I believe the information is important and totally relevant to learning and applying the art of project management and so, I am including it here in toto.

Early in my career I came into possession of a slim, black, hardcover book titled, *The Black Book of Executive Politics* by Z. I never bothered to investigate to find out who "Z" really is. Regardless, I have found the contents of the book very helpful and the author includes a couple of very useful tactics that I feel compelled to share when discussion office politics and the art of project management. Although the book is written to help the corporate climber, my dissection of the book is entirely through the lens of the art of project management.

The author states that s/he advocates, "… getting things done by throwing out an overblown, overly polite, crippling world view that keeps most of today's executives tripping over themselves to avoid offending other people. I advocate acting aggressively and effectively." My experience has borne out what Z says. To be an effective project manager, we cannot be effective while being afraid to offend someone. Don't get me wrong, cutting a path high, wide, and deep through the emotional lives of your stakeholders and project team will likely sink you. However, there are times and places where you need to speak the truth clearly and plainly regardless of whose feelings get hurt, and let the chips fall where they may. Typically, the time for this kind of frank talk is when the failure to speak will probably cause failure of the project.

Polity is usually a form of oil which keeps relationships moving smoothly. However, when overblown, it actually creates dysfunctional relationships and often results in rampant passive-aggressive behaviors and, when widespread in an organization, a passive-aggressive corporate culture.

Aggressive and assertive behavior are separated by a thin line. While aggression is usually a negative emotion and pretty consistently produces negative results both in yourself and your environment, assertiveness is a very necessary element for a well-balanced person and for your emotional well-being. Whenever possible, stay on the assertive side of that line between the two. If you don't know the difference between the two, then make it a subject of study to learn the differences and to cultivate assertiveness. The following link will take you to a whole list of materials available at Amazon to help you learn more about assertiveness and how to make it a part of your routine (and healthy) behaviors: _Assertiveness Books_, _Assertiveness Audios_.

Your Political Roadmap – Z teaches how to effectively use a corporate organizational chart.
1. Identify the key people you know you will need to work with.

2. Use a large sheet of paper (or a drawing program) and put the names of the highest-ranking people in row across the top of the page. (if you have more than 25 names, you may need to do a separate sheet for each name).
3. Put a circle around each name with enough space in the circle for you to enter comments.
4. Below each name, write the names of the people who report to them and continue on down past your own organizational level so that there is room for one or two levels below you.
5. In each circle, write your impressions of that person, the type of relationship you have with him or her, common interests you share, and potential areas of conflict you have.
6. Draw blue lines between each circle to represent formal reporting relationships between the people on your chart(s).
7. Draw red lines between each circle to indicate any strong personal or political alliances you have discovered or perceived between people.
8. On each each reporting line, make notes of one or two key facts about the reporting relationship. Be prepared to change these notes as facts or your information changes.
9. On each of the alliance lines make similar notes. Change these notes as situations evolve.
10. Update your political road map every week.
11. Never leave your road map where anyone else can find it.

On point #5 above, when you note your common interests, realize that your common interests can be used to help you build rapport and support with these people. Support which may prove critical to your ability to navigate yourself and your project to success. Here are a few potential common interests to consider:

- Beliefs and interests – Political, moral, religious, spiritual or other beliefs. Hobbies, sports and other interests.
- Heritage – Although discriminating against someone for their heritage can land you in the middle of a lawsuit, taking advantage of your cultural, religious, racial or

national backgrounds when building alliances is just plain smart.
- Education and schooling – Alumni of your alma mater can prove invaluable allies. Others with a similar educational background may help you uncover unknown blindspots or skills you may be neglecting that you need to refresh.
- Appearance – Don't be a slob. Look at the successful and influential people in the organization and emulate their level of dress and appearance. This simple approach is surprisingly effective in building rapport.
- Language – do you have a second, or third language in common with key players? Use it to build ties with others who speak the same language.
- Community – do you live in the same neighborhood, belong to the same social organizations?
- Family – Are you biologically or martially related to any of these players?
- Possessions – do you share common interests in specific kinds or models of objects, e.g., fine art, cars, books, etc.?
- Personality – Do you have a similar or sympathetic personality with a key player, e.g., funny, cynical, skeptical, grumpy, etc.?
- Style – Are you a jock, a chic dresser? Similarities in appearance and style can be easy points to use silently and swiftly build rapport.

A word about your personality and personal style. While all of us can benefit from improvement, and our personality and personal style are not immutable, before you attempt to change these aspects of yourself to fit an organization consider why you are the way you are.

If your personal style and personality are the result of deeply held beliefs, rather than just whims or reactions to events in your life, then do not change or relinquish them lightly or to fit in. When you find your way of thinking, your style makes you feel like a fish out of water in your organization, you are in the wrong organization.

For many years I have coached people on job searching and

career success. I have repeatedly warned them that during the interview process, they need to get an idea of the corporate culture, the team culture and the management style of those they might be working with. If it conflicts sharply with their own preferred way of life or approach to conflict or issues, then they should politely decline any job offers and keep looking for a company environment where they will more likely fit in. To do otherwise is nearly a guarantee that a new job search will be coming very shortly, and it may have a hostile work relationship driving it.

When considering the people in your corporate power diagram, don't make rash conclusions. Do your homework to confirm any initial conclusions and try to confirm your conclusions with people who are well-acquainted with the people in your chart. Don't limit your confirmations to those within the current organization. Find out where they have worked before and what they did there.

As data comes in, hone your observations and notes on your power diagram. Develop a robust picture of the responsibilities, reporting lines, interests and activities of each person.

Finally, consider the person's age and their tenure in the organization. While young bucks (and does) may make a big splash and garner lots of attention, the gray hairs often are accompanied with extensive connections, information and informal power. Cultivating these assets can often be easier than building relationships with younger people. The old hands are often more than willing to share their knowledge and connections with someone who shows a respectful interest in them.

Z mentions several political mistakes which will likely sink you. Making one or more of these faux pas may make it impossible for you to succeed in your organization, in any role.

- Timing – Asking for support before you have established a firm relationship. Or, to put it in terms that Stephen R Covey uses in his book, *The 7 Habits of Highly Effective People* – seeking to withdraw from the relationship bank account before you have made sufficient deposits.
- Stepping on toes – When you unwittingly propose things, or make statements, that diminish the power or prestige of

another person, you usually make an enemy. When that person is a key figure in your power diagram, likely you will find the entire weight of power represented in that diagram brought to bear to help see you humiliated and pushed out the door.

- Foundationless alliances or overusing an alliance – in both of these cases you are again drawing on a relationship-bank-account where you haven't yet built up a sufficient balance to prevent an overdraft.
- Posturing – When you infer knowledge, power or influence that you don't actually have you might win, but you run a very, very high risk that someone will either call your bluff, or simply uncover the truth and expose you for a fraud. And, once others know you for a fraud, your credibility, your effectiveness, and your support will evaporate like fog on a hot day.
- Neglecting alliances – Just because you had a close relationship with someone in the past does not mean the strength of that relationship is just as strong today. Make the time to keep your relationships strong so that you can use them with confidence when necessary. And strengthen them well before the time you need them.

Another key point Z makes is that you cannot afford to underestimate any opponents you face. And any competent project manager will have opponents. Sometimes even your allies can look like opponents.

Here are some key indicators of the clout someone else may have:

- Membership on key corporate committees.
- Connections – has management above them changed recently? A key umbrella of support may have been taken away.
- Staff – how many people does this person supervise directly and indirectly? Has this number gone up or down dramatically in recent years?
- Positioning – Where is the organization headed relative to the position this person holds? Was she just put in charge

of Buggy-whip operations as the company moves into manufacturing cars?
- Personality – chances are if you find someone unpleasant, upper management and others will too.

Z points out several personality types to beware of, as they can disrupt or sabotage you completely. Some may do this simply to prove they can, others because they are jealous or want your position. When considering your interactions with these people remember the story of the frog and the scorpion. When the scorpion eventually stings the helpful frog and the frog asks, "why?" The scorpions responds that is just his nature. If you deal with these people in ignorance, you will end up with regrets. When you deal with them will full knowledge of what they are, you can find ways to turn their nature to your advantage (making sure you aren't the frog).

- Self-aggrandizers – these people are "legends in their own minds." Look carefully at the accomplishments and relationships people claim and seek confirmation of those things. When you find significant discrepancies between actual and claimed power, accomplishments and relationships, you can know that you need not take them too seriously and should not rely upon them.
- Insinuators – these are real scorpions who are looking for the opportunity to do you in. They may bring you "inside" information that leads you to believe that things are better, or worse, than you believe. They may offer to help you fix the problem while claiming credit for your work, or outright sabotaging your efforts by misleading you. Confronting or "outing" insinuators doesn't work to your advantage. You need avoid them and let their deceits come out in the natural course of events.
- Strategists – these folks may mislead you or lull you into a false sense of security so that they can rush ahead and make your performance look slow by comparison. Rather than reacting to these folks, and going faster or slower, do your work at your pace. Don't be rushed into producing

hasty work, or lulled into taking longer than you can to produce quality work.
- Bullies – people who try to bulldoze over you or intimidate you may have a variety of motivations. Your best defense is to assess how much power they really have and make strategic decisions to either stand your ground or yield, depending on what will produce the best results for you and your project.

Don't leave your opinions at the door. A common failure made by project managers is to always defer to others and never take a stand or voice an opinion of their own. Although there are times when you need to remember the first rule of business, "The customer is always right." In spite of that you may need to remind your customer that s/he is paying good money for your experience and expertise and their disregard for your opinion or viewpoint may be wasting that investment.

If you judge that the difference in opinion between you and the customer is going to result in the abject failure of the project, you may need to remember the third rule of business, "Although the customer is always right, they may not be your customer."

When you consider invoking the third rule of business, it means that you feel strongly enough about the direction the customer is headed that you are prepared to separate yourself from the project (and perhaps the organization). This is not a step to be taken lightly, because it can easily land you in the unemployment line. You need to be prepared for the consequences of invoking this option. If you aren't willing to pay the price, then refer to the second rule of business, "when the customer is wrong, refer to rule #1."

Z goes on to discuss persuasion, risk management, negotiation, using discord, when to break the rules, resisting manipulation, reprimanding, manipulating without alienating, as well as some basic do's and don'ts of the office, e.g., drinking, office sex, etc. Also included is handling the press, delivering bad news without getting "shot", hiring friends, knowing when to make an exit, and many other topics. On each of these, the author devotes from a few paragraphs to a few pages. While the tidbits are useful and spot-on, they are too tangential to the art of project management for me to list and elaborate on here.

I suppose, having devoted several thousand words to this review, it goes without saying that I highly recommend this book. While not all the lessons are on-the-nose for the art of project management, they are definitely relevant for anyone who is trying to move up a corporate ladder. As a contractor / consultant, moving up the corporate ladder is not a prime consideration for me. However, being aware of everything in this book allows me to avoid getting unwittingly caught crosswise of any climbers who may be involved, or even in the organizational neighborhood of the projects I run. I believe you will find this equally true for yourself. And, if you are a PM now, but want to eventually land a full-time gig in the upper reaches of a company, the lessons in this slim volume will prove invaluable.

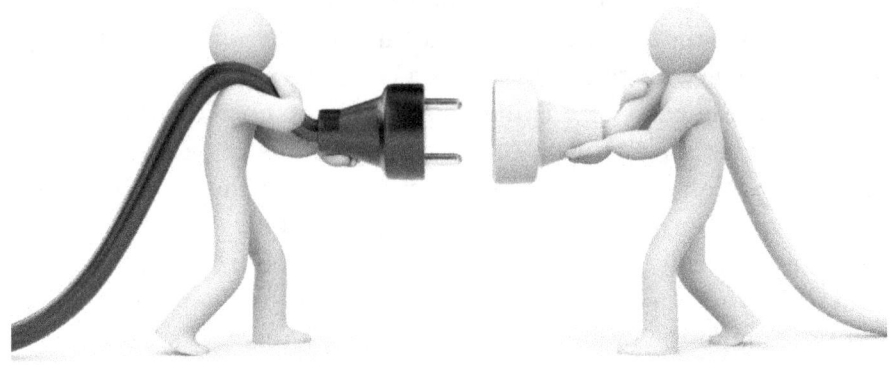

© Copyright 2017 by @ Pixelery.com, Image used with permission through DepositPhotos.com

## CHAPTER 12: THE LAWS OF POWER FOR THE PM

"To some people the notion of consciously playing power games ... seems evil. ... They believe they can opt out of the game by behaving in ways that have nothing to do with power."

Robert Greene<br>The 48 Laws of Power

The reality is that the approach Mr. Greene mentions above is naïve at best, career suicide at worst, and is most likely, according to Mr. Greene, no more than a clever ruse to hide the power games actually being played.

For many years I have said that I don't play power politics in organizations, but I do understand them and navigate through the them. In retrospect, that statement is not totally true. Navigating through power politics is a way of playing power politics. In fact, it is a totally necessary success technique for a skillful project manager to do the job and add value without getting derailed by organizational infighting.

Power games exist in every organization. Refusing to recognize and learn how to navigate them will condemn you to forever be a pawn for someone else in those games. Your career, and by extension your life, will be utterly out of your control. You will have surrendered your proper place at the helm of your career to be tossed and driven by every wind and current of the powers that surround you and are maneuvering for their own objectives, good or ill.

There is no nobility in eschewing the intelligent and principled use of the powers which you accrue. In point of fact, from a religious standpoint there is ample evidence to suggest that failing to use what you have correctly is a grievous sin. The Bible tells the parable of the talents wherein the person who hid the talent, instead of using and multiplying it, was punished.

However, don't equate the abuse of power with the use of power. Elsewhere in this book you can read about the correct interpretation of the Golden Rule and how its proper application would preclude you from abusing the power(s) that come to you.

> **"Instead of struggling against the inevitable, instead of arguing and whining and feeling guilty, it is far better to excel at power. In fact, the better you are at dealing with power, the better friend, lover, husband, wife, and person you become... By mastering the 48 laws in this book, you spare others the pain that comes from bungling with power—by playing with fire without knowing its properties. If the game of power is inescapable, better to be an artist than a denier or a bungler."**
>
> Robert Green, _The 48 Laws of Power_

The skillful PM may not be an artist with the all the laws of power, but s/he cannot afford to be a denier or a bungler. The reality is that a properly positioned project manager is in a position of significant power, whether or not the power is recognized.

What follows are a few more selections from the Laws of Power and my commentary on each.

**"An emotional response to a situation is the single greatest**

**barrier to power,..."**

*48 Laws of Power*

Losing your cool, or otherwise getting emotional is one of the worst mistakes you can make as a project manager. Even if your emotion is wholly justified, its manifestation reveals that you are vulnerable and can potentially be manipulated, given the right stimulus.

When something outrageous happens, and you respond emotionally, you are following the crowd instead of leading it. While others may feel your response is justified, it will always decrease their confidence in your ability to think and act clearly in all situations.

Maintaining your composure in all circumstances generates respect (and perhaps even some fear) in everyone who recognizes the fact that your words and actions are not driven about by your emotions.

**"Seek the clarity of perspective. ... distance yourself from the present moment and think objectively about the past and future."**

*The 48 Laws of Power*

Maintaining perspective is another aspect of maintaining your self-control and your influence over others, and over events around you.

There is an old saying, "you cannot see the forest for the trees." This aphorism expresses the fact that all too often we are so distracted by the events that are happening right in front of us that we fail to see the trends we are living through and how these events will appear when viewed from the perspective of physical distance.

Looking at what is happening in one company (or project) from the perspective of another company, the industry as a whole, or even from another industry can help you to see when your actions make little sense or are precisely what you should be doing.

Long ago I was taught that if I would likely be able to laugh about something five years from now, I should go ahead and laugh about it now. This notion of applying the perspective of time also applies. It is also an effective means of deescalating the emotion in various situations.

> **"Know who you are dealing with. Do not offend the wrong person."**
> 
> *The 48 Laws of Power*

The skillful project manager tries not to offend anyone. However, sometimes giving offense happens. Before it does, it is very wise to find out who you are dealing with. Elsewhere in this book is a chapter that is essentially the review of a book on executive politics.

The author of that book on executive politics provides a process which the skillful PM will follow to map out the organization and its lines of power as swiftly as possible.

If you will follow that process, you will be far less likely to unwittingly offend someone who is in a position to make life difficult for you. And, before you accuse me of some kind of snobbery, consider the fact that all too often, the person you cannot afford to offend is not the one in power, but those who appear menial, but actually control access to those in power.

If you are unaware of the connections of people in an organization, then you are dancing in a political minefield, blindfolded. The wrong word or action to the wrong person and all your venerated skills and abilities won't slow your expulsion out the door.

> **"Insecurity drives power away. Security comes from knowing both your strengths and weaknesses. Knowing what you are capable of doing allows you to avoid failure through over promising and under delivering. Security also comes from knowing the strengths and weaknesses of your team and others around you. Trying to do it all yourself is a recipe for failure. Using the skills and abilities of others effectively is a sure path to success."**
>
> *The 48 Laws of Power*

In the conclusion of this book, I present the story of Jack and Dianne. When you read that story, you will realize that Jack's failure and Dianne's triumph were directly attributable to their respective violation and adherence to this law of power.

> "Demonstrate, don't explicate. Win through actions, never through argument. Argument stirs resentment."
> *The 48 Laws of Power*

No one likes a know-it-all and no one likes to hear someone say, "I told you so." Gloating and rubbing the noses of others in the fact that you are right, all stir resentment. Argument and demonstration both risk these resentments. Of the two, demonstration is slightly less likely to cause resentment.

The best way, even better than demonstration, is to get your target to believe the idea was their own. Help them to "discover" and flesh out the idea. Then, they have the satisfaction of being "right" and you have the satisfaction of having them do what you need them to do.

Greene's 48 Laws of Power, like any truly useful tool, are both helpful and dangerous. His exposition of these laws, much like Machiavelli's advice to his "Prince", is not tempered with morality. He only explains the laws and how they can be applied to allow you to garner, use and retain power. The view in his book is that the accrual of power is the end, not the tool.

Much like authors who teach cutthroat negotiation tactics or the con man who tutors his protégé in how to deceive and defraud, there is little or no consideration given to end results of such actions and their effects on your own inner self.

The skillful project manager understands that power is a tool, not an objective in itself. Power is there to be used to deliver the project for your client while enhancing, not tearing down, your brand.

Becoming known as a ruthless but powerful person may be the reputation you desire, but it is not the reputation that will keep your clients coming to you for project after project. So, use the laws of power with good judgement, always keeping in mind that the law of the harvest is a natural law which transcends all the laws of power. You will reap what you sow, and you will become the fruits of your actions.

© 2017 albund, image used with permission through DepositPhotos.com

## CHAPTER 13: CORPORATE CULTURE TRAPS

"The culture of any organization is shaped by the worst behavior the leader is willing to tolerate."
Steve Gruenert and Todd Whitaker,
*School Culture Rewired*,
ch. 3 (2015)

Every corporation has its own culture. The culture defines what is acceptable and unacceptable behavior. Some corporate cultures are so brutal and cutthroat that you will spend half of your time just trying to avoid getting a metaphorical knife in your back and the other half making sure that the right people hear about your stellar performance. Others are so nurturing that they let people retire in place and keep so many people on the payroll past their "sell-by" date that it is nearly impossible to find anyone who can really get a job done, but you cannot jettison the dead wood from your team so that you can deliver the desired results. Both extremes are undesirable and frustrating for a project manager.

Regardless of where your client's corporate culture fits on that scale, you need to understand it so that you can navigate it and use it effectively. Knowing the norms for a corporation allows you to not only fit in, but to make an informed decision about when you need to step outside of the boundaries to achieve your objectives.

There are some aspects of corporate culture which are shaped by the culture of the nation where the company lives. Other aspects are shaped by the personalities of top managers. And, within every corporation there are pockets, large and small, where a different culture prevails. These pockets of cultural aberration (good or bad) are usually shaped by some powerful local leader. These pockets may buck the corporate trend, or they may take that culture to an extreme.

To be effective, the skillful PM will understand the corporate culture at all the levels s/he has to deal with and will generally conform to those cultural expectations. Venturing outside of those boundaries is dangerous. You may do it upon occasion when dramatic action is needed. However, every day you operate outside of the norms is a day of significantly escalated risk for your continued participation in the project. Even a flawless execution of the project may not be sufficient to keep you on when you operate for too long outside of the normally acceptable boundaries of the prevailing corporate culture.

**Beware of Snowflakes** – The most common trap of corporate culture that I have seen is what I call the snowflake syndrome. It can be a powerful inhibitor against making progress or innovation happen, and it can create enough of a chill on your efforts to get you shown the door if you don't navigate through the issue correctly.

We have all been taught that every snowflake is unique from every other snowflake.

Many organizations sustain an unspoken (or sometimes spoken) belief that their organization is unique in so many ways that an outsider cannot quickly, easily or effectively add value. Warning signs of these organizations are a shortage of subject matter experts (SMEs) or a very long anticipated learning curve before a new hire is expected to become productive in their job. Another warning sign can be lots of gray hair. When all the experts have been there for ten years or more and are the only experts available, you may be looking at a snowflake culture.

What our school teachers failed to teach us, or we failed to learn, is that snowflakes have much more in common with each other than they are dissimilar. For instance, snowflakes are typically formed from a little water and some dust. They begin to form in the 30 to 34 degrees Fahrenheit temperature range, and they melt in the same temperature range. Although each shape is distinct, each has six sides.

### What do snowflakes and corporate cultures have in common?

When a snowflake culture prevails in an organization, it is hard for members and units in that organization to believe and acknowledge that outsiders, even in their own industry, can come in and quickly understand enough of the current way things are done to offer meaningful insights into how they work and how they could work better.

### Snowflakes can bury you in an avalanche of resistance.

When you find yourself in a world of snowflakes, you can either retreat to a job with a company where reality prevails, you can set yourself to joust windmills like Don Quixote, or you can work to quietly disprove the snowflake syndrome assumptions on a case by case basis.

Jousting windmills can be fun for a while, and you may actually make some progress here and there, but the probabilities are against your success. Your most likely avenue for success lies in retreat. However, if you are a glutton for punishment and enjoy pounding your head against brick walls, you might enjoy limited victories by demonstrating in limited cases where outside help and perspectives yield superior results to abject reliance on the home grown SMEs.

Bear in mind, however, that as you battle, or even worse – succeed, in revealing the absurdity of the snowflake mentality, you are assaulting the foundations of job security for these snowflakes. That threat will not be taken lightly and some will go to any lengths to sink you in order to protect their jobs.

The most terrible irony here is that as the snowflakes succeed in burying change agents like you, they move their company one step closer towards inevitable destruction and the loss of their own jobs. The marketplace is such a rapidly changing place that any organization which fails to learn and adapt will eventually either collapse or get consumed by more nimble rivals.

Still you can be right, and unemployed at the same time. So, you must decide how to act when you are faced with a large group of snowflakes in the workplace. Being unemployed does nothing to enhance your reputation for delivering quality results. But, delivering quality results in the face of resistance from a snowflake culture adds one more, very substantial, risk factor in the path of your project.

© Copyright 2017 by @ jogg2002, Image used with permission through DepositPhotos.com

## CHAPTER 14: PROJECT IMPACTS

"There are a thousand hacking at the branches of [a problem] to one who is striking at the root.."

Thoreau (paraphrased)

Failure to understand the project objective(s) and impact(s) on the organization can be a career-ending mistake.

The skillful PM looks for the root causes that gave birth to the project. Uncovering those root causes, often reveals a misguided project, one that will ultimately result in the waste of corporate time and resources. And, when the project fails to deliver the desired results, the most convenient scapegoat for the failure is the project manager.

This attributed guilt and bad judgement is not entirely unjustified. As a project expert, the PM should be able to see past the noise and dust surrounding a project and correctly evaluate whether or not a project is treating symptoms or root causes.

The realignment or ending of a project is often perilous because of the project sponsors. They have invested their political and corporate capital in promoting the project and, even if you are right, pointing out their failure is almost certain to end in your own dismissal and failure.  So, the skillful PM must carefully help the project sponsors (both formal and informal sponsors) to discover the error of their ways while making it appear that they realized that all on their own, rather than having you point it out to them.

Once the error is seen, you can help them to either end the project or to navigate its transformation into what will actually address the root causes of the problem the project is supposed to resolve.

When a project fails to meets its objectives or has significant, unforeseen impacts, corporate management will always blame the project manager.  The sponsor may also get the axe, but the PM will definitely have a black mark on his or her resume.    John Georgius was the COO of First Union National Bank, one of the ten largest banks in the US.  In the early 1994 his boss, Ed Crutchfield, commissioned a study which revealed the future of retail banking would involve customers who fell into several distinct categories as consumers of banking services.

- Some customers would want to use the teller for nearly everything, doing face-to-face banking almost exclusively.
- Other customers would want to use Internet banking or phones almost exclusively.
- Some would rely almost entirely on ATMs.
- A few would want to use a mix of ATMs and Tellers and the Internet.

Crutchfield devised a strategy known as Future Bank to redesign the entire bank to align with these new customer segments.  As part of this Future Bank initiative, not only would bank branches and jobs be totally revised, customers would be forced to choose one of these four packages of services.  Going outside the limits of these services would incur additional fees.  For instance, the Internet banking customer would have to pay a fee if they actually visited a bank branch and interacted with a teller.

The changes promoted to the bank culture were dramatic as well.  The traditional banking service model was being thrown over the side and replaced with an aggressive, sales-oriented culture, including a commission-only sales force tasked with cold-calling middle market customers to sell them bank, brokerage and insurance services.

Georgius was named President of the Bank, while Crutchfield relinquished the title and held on as Chairman of the Board of Directors. Georgius was effectively the sponsor and project lead for Future Bank, the actual PM was kept in the shadows for this high-risk, high-profile project.

In the midst of implementing this strategy, First Union bought CoreStates Bank. As part of the acquisition, CoreStates bankers and customers would be pushed into these rigid service approaches and aggressive sales culture.

The result was a wholesale rebellion which manifested itself in customer defections that far exceeded expectations of normal runoff during a merger. In addition, employees of Core States, profoundly unhappy with the merger, and further aggravated by this rigid approach, engaged in acts of sabotage which further alienated Core States customers from First Union.

Compounding the financial problems from the CoreStates acquisition, the purchase of the sub-prime lender The Money Store added the debacle of a bad acquisition to the problems of these faulty implementations of strategy.

The end results cost First Union dearly in terms of significantly lower returns from the acquisition than they had ever before experienced with an acquisition as well as a huge reputational loss in the market place.

In November 1999, Georgius was involuntarily retired and Future Bank was shelved. Chairman of the Board Ed Crutchfield named Ken Thompson as the new President, and the Future Bank initiative was quietly killed. The PM in charge would never want to claim that role in Future Bank on his resume.

While the original plan and idea had been Crutchfield's, and the acquisitions approved by him as well, it was the front-man Georguis who took the fall for the failure. His banking career was ended, his financial reputation irredeemably tarnished by this massive failure.

Today, most banking customers fit into one of those categories predicted in the original study. But they moved there on their own, not by being forced to choose as part of a project plan. The intent of the project had been to position the business for efficiency and effectiveness in the banking world of the future. The impact of the project was lost customers, lost stock value, and damage to the name of First Union which prompted it to shed the tarnished First Union name in their last major acquisition, Wachovia.

The failure to foresee the impacts of the Future Bank project, to see beyond the noise and the dust, cost First Union hundreds of millions of dollars. It cost them customers. It cost them many loyal and competent employees. It cost them time and distracted them from capitalizing on their strengths during the critical activities associated with the evaluation of The Money Store and the integration of CoreStates.

The fact that many of the parts of Future Bank are now ordinary parts of the consumer banking world is cold consolation to Georgius others who lost their jobs when the unforeseen impacts of the Future Bank project overwhelmed the successful portions of their effort.

## CHAPTER 15: CONSTRUCTIVE CONFLICT

"A good manager doesn't try to eliminate conflict' he tries to keep it from wasting the energies of his people. If you're the boss and your people fight you openly when they think you are wrong – that's healthy."

Robert Townsend

All too often when people think of conflict, they only have a negative view. They imagine only strife, anger, wounded feelings, and destructive interactions. However, the reality of conflict, when managed correctly is increased productivity, superior results, and more effective teamwork.

I am not alone in this view of conflict. Wikipedia asserts that <u>*conflict management*</u> is the process of limiting the negative aspects of conflict while increasing the positive aspects.

# The Art of Project Management

The 100% negative view of conflict leads us to employ strategies for conflict avoidance and suppression. The skillful project manager understands that conflict, like risk, is not only inevitable, but when used correctly can be the catalyst for superior results.

Most people know that the four stages of team formation are forming, norming, storming and performing. Likewise, many people know that anger is one of the seven stages of grief. In spite of knowing these things, they do their utmost to suppress, avoid, or prevent anger. Anger and "storming" are tightly bound to conflict and moving through that anger and storming or conflict is a necessary step for growth. Unfortunately, the result of these kind of conflict suppression and avoidance is a retardation of the emotional maturity of the project team.

The skillful PM knows how to draw the conflict to the surface as early as possible in the project life cycle. Once surfaced, the conflict is acknowledged and managed. It is used to create a better product and to get greater commitment to the success of the project, even from those who were initially opposed to the work.

One of the easiest ways to surface and channel conflict that I have found is using a combined exercise which involves a force field analysis along with an high level risk assessment. In the force field analysis portion of the exercise, the project team members are asked to brainstorm both why the project should be done, and why it should not be done. They are asked what could prevent this project from succeeding.

Usually, the participants are very willing to talk about why the project should be done, but may feel reluctant to voice their objections to the project. However, once you get them started on the negatives, they will unleash a very energetic torrent of objections and point out everything that can go wrong.

Every pro and con gets written on the board. And in the writing lies some of the power of this exercise. Simply acknowledging the possible failure points and objections publicly lets participants know that their concern has been heard.

The next part of the exercise is to determine what can be done in the project to keep from having those bad things happen. Surprisingly those who put forth the objections are often the most vocal in offering ways to prevent these obstacles or to overcome them if they do arise.

Voicing their objections, and then seeing countermeasures they have suggested put into action within the project gives the objectors "skin in the game." They have now offered up their intellectual capital to help the project succeed, and they don't want to be proven wrong about how they imagined the bad things can be countered.

This one exercise is often enough to totally transform the project team and its official sponsors (and opponents) into a team that is dedicated to seeing the project succeed.

*Experts* note that there are five general approaches to conflict management: Competing, Compromising, Collaborating, Avoiding, and Accommodating . The skillful PM is familiar with each of these approaches and uses each, effectively when appropriate.

It is worth noting that conflict management does not imply conflict resolution. Rather than being focused on eliminating conflict (via resolution), conflict management is about using conflict constructively to ensure that the right questions get asked and ideas challenged so that the project has the best possible chance of succeeding and providing the intended benefits.

**Competing-** When competing, an individual pursues his or her own concerns at the other person's expense, using whatever power seems appropriate to win his or her position. Competing might mean standing up for your rights, defending a position you believe is correct, or simply trying to win.

**Compromising** – it has been said that the art of comprise consists in making sure that no one got everything they wanted, everyone got something they wanted, and everyone is approximately equally discontent with the solution.

While this view is a bit negative, it is not wrong. Most often comprise is the basis for building consensus. And consensus building is a key tool used by the skillful PM when several parties have conflicting interests which intersect your project.

**Collaborating** – This is trying to seek a win-win solution where you are trying to find a solution that fully meets everyone's needs.

To succeed, each party must bring forward their true concerns, not just put forward negotiating positions. When the parties involved are fully forthcoming, the skillful PM identifies those situations and works privately to unearth the real needs and finds ways to help each party articulate those needs in the negotiation in ways that doesn't embarrass, humiliate or weaken a party.

The skillful PM also asks pertinent questions to reveal differing and common views of elements affecting the negotiation. This helps uncover the motives and perspectives which can often derail negotiations when they are not understood.

**Avoiding** – Some experts interpret conflict avoidance as either a passive-aggressive approach to conflict or as simply unassertive. My experience has been that it can be either or neither of those.

The manager who walks away from a negotiation may do it with the words, "take it or leave it" either ringing in his ears or coming out of his mouth is typically being very aggressive.

The negotiator who insists on win-win-or-walk-away is being very assertive.

While I am typically of the view that the sooner conflict is addressed, the better. I also know that there are times when the best solution is to defer a confrontation. Sometimes, time will resolve the issue for you. At other times, you need to avoid the conflict until you are fully prepared to address it with facts and a cool head.

**Accommodating** – Accommodation is typically seen as the opposite of competing, but to my view it is simply a variant of conflict avoidance. When you accommodate, you will often be neglecting or ignoring your own needs or concerns while meeting the needs, concerns or demands of others in the interests of avoiding further conflict.

At Appomattox Courthouse in 1865 when General U.S. Grant demanded the unconditional surrender of the forces of Robert E. Lee, in order to avoid any further conflict, Lee accommodated those that demand and surrendered without attempting to gain any concessions.

Likewise at the end of World War II when the Emperor of

Japan came on board the deck of the Battleship USS Missouri it was to avoid further conflict and accommodate the demand of the US for unconditional surrender.

In spite of those historical examples it is worth repeating that conflict management is not synonymous with conflict resolution.

The unconditional surrender of Lee at Appomattox, while it resolved the issue of the rights of states to secede from the union, and it sealed the fate of slavery in the US, it did not end the conflict between slave owners and either their opponents or victims. That conflict continued to play out through the Civil Rights Era of the 1960s and to a much lesser extent in our society today.

Likewise, when Emperor Tojo submitted to unconditional surrender in Tokyo Bay, it did not resolve the conflicts over resources which led the Japanese into war in the first place. That conflict too continues to play out on the world stage. To some degree, in the post-war rebuilding of Japan and their subsequent use of the advantages gained through their rebuilding (all made possible by their accommodation at the treaty table) the Japanese have arguable gained every goal they set out to attain in World War II. They now have amazing access to world markets for their goods and are as unfettered in their access to natural resources as any other trading country in the world.

In like manner, accommodation in negotiations does not mean that the conflict is resolved. In fact, it will likely subsequently reappear in some other form. That is why when the skillful PM is seeking to negotiate and resolve conflict, the ability to use principled negotiation (mentioned elsewhere in this book) is essential.

© Copyright 2017 by @ Olivier26, Image used with permission through DepositPhotos.com

## CHAPTER 16: USING STRESS

*"Times of great calamity and confusion have been productive for the greatest minds. The purest ore is produced from the hottest furnace. The brightest thunder-bolt is elicited from the darkest storm."*

Charles Caleb Colton

Stress is usually considered a problem. The skillful PM recognizes that stress is a powerful tool which can be used to motivate people to deliver the results you need, when you want them. However, like any power tool, unmanaged stress will destroy and undermine your efforts.

Stress takes two broad forms: Eustress and Distress. Eustress is a positive form of stress while distress is negative stress. Most of us use the term "stress" to refer exclusively to distress.

Eustress, or positive stress, has several identifying characteristics:

- Motivates, focuses energy.
- Is short-term.

- Is perceived as within our coping abilities.
- Feels exciting.
- Improves performance.

Distress, in contrast, is characterized by:
- Causes anxiety or concern.
- Can be short- or long-term.
- Is perceived as outside of our coping abilities.
- Feels unpleasant.
- Decreases performance.
- Can lead to mental and physical problems.

Note that distress and eustress are not differentiated by their causes, rather these characteristics describe our reaction to events. In short, whether a person experiences distress or eustress depends entirely on their reaction to the stressor, and it is not dependent on the nature of the stressor itself.

From my view, the key to differentiating distress from eustress lies in the notion of whether or not we believe the stressor is within our coping abilities or not. This notion is essential for understanding how to use stress, on yourself and others, to get done what you want, and what the project requires.

To a significant degree, successful PMs thrive somewhat on stress. Deadlines drive them. The closer a deadline looms the more energy and commitment they bring to the work. Skillful project managers know how to internally channel stress to help them achieve their best, because they know their strengths and weaknesses as well as the capabilities of their team.

The truly skillful PM knows how to stress others to help them achieve their best. Often, this involves helping your team members to realize or gain the abilities they need to accomplish the task(s) at hand.

When the work required appears to be beyond the coping abilities of your team member(s), you need to be able to realistically assess each member of your team and determine either who has the ability to do the work, or who has the ability to be trained to do the work the way it needs to be done. In most cases, there are people on your team who can deliver what you need if you give them the right knowledge / training and some incentive.

If you have already built their loyalty, you won't have to offer explicit, up-front incentives or blandishments. They will already know that when they do right by you, you will do right by them.

All that to one side, there will be times when you will need to ratchet up the pressure (stress) on your team. Sometimes without the benefit of knowing them very well.

I gained a reputation with one client as a project manager who could get projects "out of the ditch" and back on track. That led to me being called in to pick up a particular project that had fallen behind schedule and was at risk of not delivering at all.

I brought together the project team for my first meeting and, after brief introductions and a situation report, I told them all to take out their phones and calendars and to start making calls to cancel all their planned meetings, evening and weekend activities for the next three weeks. I informed them that for the next three weeks we were going to work whatever hours were needed to get this project delivered on time.

As you can imagine, I was not a very popular guy at that moment. And, I had some rather tense conversations with the managers of some of those folks. Interestingly enough, we didn't end up having to work nights and weekends and we did deliver the project on time, with the expected benefits to the business.

Before walking in the room for that meeting, I had already looked at the team and the plan. I had determined that the team had everything they needed to get the job done. Apparently the only thing they lacked was a sufficient sense of urgency. My requirement that they drop everything else, work and personal, was sufficient to focus their energies and get the work done.

In short, I stressed the team. The nature of the stress I applied undoubtedly produced some emotional distress. Regardless, because they were capable of doing the work, the extra stress I applied motivated them to rise to the occasion.

I was able to reward their performance by not requiring them to work evenings and weekends. Then, they earned the reward of being recognized for delivering the project by the deadline.

Deliberately stressing people is not a very "nice" thing to do. Regardless, it is often necessary. If you want to be liked all the time, being an effective project manager is not the work for you.

The skillful PM knows that not everyone is going to like you. Not everyone is going to want to work with you (before, during or after the project). While you can be friendly with members of your project team (see the chapter on Influence), you cannot be their friend. If you want friendship, don't look for it in people who you have to lead.

I am fortunate to be able to say that of all the people I have led on project teams 96% of them are willing to work with me on subsequent project teams. I don't know how many of that 96% like me or dislike me. The fact that they have confidence in my abilities and are willing to follow me in the next project is what is most important to me.

My father used to joke that the reason people become masochists is because it feels so good when it quits hurting. I don't know if that is true or not about masochists. But, I do know there is an element of truth to this in regards to stress.

The skillful application of stress and its timely decrease or cessation can be a powerful tool for both motivation and reward. Done well, the skillful PM will be viewed as an effective stress-reducer, even when s/he is the very person ratcheting up the stress.

Being able to motivate people is closely aligned with the notion of being able to stress them in ways that produce positive results. When you understand what is most valued by each individual member of your team, you will understand how to motivate them by either giving them what they value or setting up a situation where their failure will result in depriving them of what they value.

When I told that project team to cancel all their other activities, I neither knew, nor cared what those activities were. However, I was certain that whatever they had planned to fill up their evenings and weekends was something that they valued. In that circumstance, I didn't have the opportunity to get to know each of them well enough to tailor my approach individually, so I had to apply the tyranny of equality and hope that my assumptions about their extracurricular activities were correct. The threat of loss was sufficient to generate both peer pressure and internal pressure to get the job done.

The Art of Project Management

© Copyright 2017 by @ trueffelpix, Image used with permission through DepositPhotos.com

## CHAPTER 17: PERSUASION

*"Advertising is fundamentally persuasion and persuasion happens to be not a science, but an art."*
William Bernbach

Negotiation and persuasion are both arts, rather than science. This is not to say that there is no science to support these skills. Rather, it means that anytime you are dealing with the reactions of human beings, you are dealing with an irrational, illogical situation, because human beings are never wholly rational or logical. That emotional wildcard is why so these two skills are art, rather than science.

When managing big, high-profile, high-risk projects the skills of negotiation and persuasion are integral to what you do almost on a daily basis.

In any enterprise there are typically many projects happening at any given time. In addition to these competing efforts, there is the need to carry out business-as-usual activities. Any and all of these things can adversely impact your project. And, when those adverse impacts appear on your radar, hopefully long before the actual impacts are manifested, the skillful project manager will take immediate action to reduce the risks.

The softest response to an emerging threat to the success of your project is to persuade the tougher response is to negotiate. The strongest response is to escalate the risk.

Persuasion uses many tools, all to achieve the end of getting someone else to do what you want, when you want it. Robert Cialdini has written probably one of the best books on the art of persuasion. He explores several key tactics of persuasion which every skillful PM should understand and master.

Cialdini explains six simple, but extremely powerful tactics of persuasion. The skillful PM will master using these and become acutely aware of them so that you cannot have them used on you without your consent.

**1) Little commitment – big commitment, or, the law of consistency.** Ralph Waldo Emerson is credited with saying, "consistency is the hobgoblin of a small mind." However, that is a misquote. What he actually said was, "a foolish consistency is the hobgoblin of a small mind."
The principle of persuasion Cialdini calls consistency is in fact the tactic of using a small commitment to gain a bigger commitment, all through a subtle appeal to the principle of consistency.

Inconsistent behavior is a sign of mental or emotional instability. All of us like to believe that our behaviors are consistent with our values and beliefs. We often flatter ourselves that our actions are rational, logical. In fact, they are usually almost anything but rational. In fact, they are mostly emotional.

The skillful PM knows that people, even rational people like engineers, are as emotional and irrational as everyone else. We use the principle of consistency to get our clients to make a small commitment first. This initial commitment is used to establish the pattern of consistency, which we leverage to get a larger commitment.

If we have a client who is resisting a course of action which will move our project forward, consistency is a powerful tool to bring the client to support the more dramatic action necessary.

First, you get the client to commitment to engage in some small activity, an inexpensive proof of concept, which allows you to demonstrate some value to the client. Then, you praise the client for their acumen in supporting the proof of concept and position them to sponsor the larger, more critical effort. Sometimes you have to step the client through a series of increasingly larger commitments to position them where backing out of the critical commitment would make them appear inconsistent and illogical.

**2) Reciprocity, or I'll scratch your back if you scratch mine.** The power of this principle of influence hinges on the fact that most people feel a sense of obligation if someone does a favor for them. This principle is also evident in the negotiation tactic of making a concession. You make a concession and your "opponent" feels obligated to make a corresponding concession.

The skillful project manager will find simple, effective ways to proactively do favors for those you want to influence. Thus, putting them emotionally in debt to you, making them more inclined to do something you ask of them.

Using this approach in combination with others (such as consistency & commitment) provides a powerful mechanism to build your influence with others.

A master manipulator I know teaches his students to be highly effective at networking with the rich and powerful by using reciprocity. He teaches his students to "give to get." In this case, he teaches then to find out what is valued by their target and then find ways to add value in that realm without asking for anything in return. He correctly notes that after a while, the target you are trying to influence will willingly come to you wanting to do something to help you in return for all the value you have brought to them.

Reciprocation can be used effectively to influence upwards, sideways, and downwards in your organization. I have found it to be an invaluable tool in building loyalty from my team members and loyalty is a significant help with trying to build high-performing teams.

The skillful PM is also aware of when others are attempting to use reciprocity (or any of the other tools of influence). If you are not aware of others using this tool on you, soon, you will find yourself influenced and led by them, instead of the other way around. And that will rarely bode well for your project or your reputation.

**3) Social Proofs, or, everyone is doing it.** This powerful tactics can be used to keep people in line, or to get them to get out of the line.

What effect would it have on you if your boss called you into her office and pointed out some remark you made, following it with, "In this company, we don't talk like that?" If it didn't cause you to give serious reflection on your behavior, you wouldn't be human.

However, what if the boss' admonition was in counterpoint to many times you had heard others talk exactly like that? Now, you would find yourself torn between the desire to conform to the norm you had seen versus the norm which your boss said was acceptable.

As a skillful PM, you can use this tactic to keep rogue players in line, as well as to influence leaders to accept change.

When you find an organization is doing something ineffective or inefficient and the response when you mention this practice is, "we've always done it that way," you are encountering the resistance born from social proofs.

Introducing change in the guise of "Industry Best Practices" is your way of using social proof to influence your client to change from what they have always done to a new, better way. It also has the added benefit of building your own credibility as someone who is keeping up with the latest and best innovations happening in the industry.

Using industry best practices is one of the safest ways for you to use the principle of social proofs to buck the corporate culture and influence your client to support what you need them to do.

Sending your targets "articles of interest" is another way to use social proof to influence them. When you see articles in journals, books or periodicals which reinforce the direction you need your target to move, copy them and send them to the person you are trying to influence.

Make sure that not all the articles are on this single topic or your ploy will be unmasked as a blatant move at manipulation. Instead, send some on less relevant topics which you reasonably believe may be of interest to your subject(s).

I have used this "articles of interest" tactic many times to influence leadership teams, individual performers and everyone in between. Sometimes I used it to help build my credibility. At other times I used it to subtly train my team into new ways of thinking.

Regardless of my immediate, or long-term, objective the results have been consistent. By providing third-party evidence that others are going down this same road, it reduces the need for your target to rely wholly upon their belief in your personal expertise to start moving that direction. And, your having provided the fodder (or trail of breadcrumbs) that brought them to consider this view, positions you as the go-to person or expert to help make it happen.

**4) Liking, or Beauty is a Beast.** Liking is a persuasive tool that is almost univerDianne used, with varying levels of skill. It's most simple embodiment is the proven fact that people are more amenable and well-disposed toward attractive people. But, it doesn't stop there.
Cialdini notes that

- friendliness,
- similarity,
- compliments,
- contact & cooperation,
- conditioning & association

All are part of the influencing tool he calls liking. Each of these tools are also used by the skillful PM to lead and influence others to do what is needed to successfully implement the project.

Back to the topic of beauty. Not all of us are Baywatch babes and hunks. If you are one, then good for you. Don't be afraid to use that God-given (or surgically enhanced) attractiveness to win friends and influence people. You can probably skip the next few paragraphs that only apply to those of us who never stood a chance at a career as a supermodel.

Beauty is a beast if you aren't beautiful. Unless you

understand the situation and the tools and use them effectively, you will always play second-fiddle to someone more attractive, and perhaps much less qualified or skillful, than you.

Without investing thousands of dollars in cosmetic surgery, there are many things you can do to make yourself more attractive to others. And making yourself more attractive is going to make them automatically more inclined to help you and support you. Pay attention to your physical hygiene and attire. I know this may sound crazy simple, but if you have bad breath or body odor, people won't want to work closely with you. If you dress like a homeless person, they won't accept you as a professional. I know it may not sound fair, and it isn't, but the reality is that people do judge a book (and a person) by its cover. If your outward appearance isn't up to par, most people won't take the time to find out what value you can really bring to the table.

Another simple thing you can do is to smile. There is an old saying, "Smile. It improves your face value." It also improves your earning power.

A sincere smile can transform an ugly face into a lovable one. It disarms others, putting them off their guard and making them more willing to cooperate with you.

Don't walk around like a smiling idiot, though. Smile when it is appropriate, most especially when meeting and greeting people. Being warm and engaging and a good conversationalist goes a long way toward overcoming any physical limitations on your beauty and makes you a more attractive human being.

**Friendliness.** For most organizations, except consulting firms, it is not cost effective to keep project managers who specialize like I do in managing large, expensive, high risk projects on permanent staff. Even if you do hire us, chances are, in a few months or years, we are going to leave in search of another challenge that is up to our skills.

Because of this transient nature, project managers tends to be outsiders. This means that when we start a project the "us versus them" tendency present in most organizations put the PM among "them." That is a significant disadvantage and one which must be eliminated as quickly and quietly as possible.

The best and simplest way to do this is to truly win over one or two key influencers in the company who are respected and well-liked, and use them as references when you call on the key members of your new team.

This implicit endorsement by someone they like will usually be enough to open the door so that you can then win over the key players and become one of the "us."

Failure to become one of "us" will almost certainly mean that you will fail as a PM. Even if the project goes on to succeed, it will likely be without you.

**Similarity, or Birds of a Feather.** The reality is that we don't automatically trust people who are different from us. An essential part of success is to earn the trust of those you work with, those you work for, and those who work for you.

Finding common ground with others is usually not too difficult. Find out what key people are interested in and what are their pastimes. If you can discover what interests your client and key stakeholders have, as well as your key teammates, then you can develop an interest and use that to build rapport.

Another similarity tactic, which doesn't require much research is to dress in a similar manner to those you want to influence.

To carry the same point even further, you can engage in "mirroring." Mirroring, when carried too far is parroting, or a parodying someone. When within the bounds of positive influence, mirroring involves employing similar speech patterns and body language to make the target of your influence subconsciously feel that the two of you are on the same wavelength.

For this to be effective, instead of insulting, you have to mirror in ways that are not so obvious that they become an artificial action on your part which calls attention to itself. Instead, it needs to be kept subtle to be effective.

**Compliments.** Yes. Compliments. Like me, perhaps you are suspicious of people who hand out compliments. Regardless, research has proven that complimenting people predisposes them to be willing to do things for you.

Although I seriously dislike the use of compliments purely to get people to do what you want them to do, it does work. I confess, I still am not very liberal with my compliments, although

I do try to find something nice I can say about everyone, even if it is solely to compliment them for the sincerity of their intentions.

Undoubtedly if you can get better at compliments than I, you will find it easier to win the cooperation of others.

**Contact & Cooperation.** As remote workers increasingly fill the workplace, and the project teams, the challenge for a skillful PM is to make meaningful contact with those whose help you need to succeed. This includes both team members, project sponsors and key resources (who may overtly or covertly oppose the project).

It is important that you find ways to make face-to-face contact with your teammates, even if it is via video conferences. Putting faces to voices, and qualifications to those people helps build rapport within the team, and it helps you become a real person to your team members.

Cooperating with others, involving them in problem solving shows that you value them and helps build their sense that they need you as well. Working your way into becoming part of the "us" group takes a real exercise in cooperation.

I worked with an executive whom I will call Ray. Ray was a very smart and experienced guy. He was hired into the company I worked for at the time to head their sales organization.

Ray developed a set of pretty remarkable products for our high net worth clients, which he attempted to roll out through the sales force.

I advised Ray that he needed to present these concepts to the sales people and ask for their input. Chances were excellent that the final product would be almost exactly what Ray had concocted.

Ray disagreed. This was his brainchild and he wanted to present it as an whole-cloth. He did it his way.

When the products rolled out, they experienced some glitches, as all new products will. Because Ray had not involved the sales team in creating the products he wasn't part of their "us." So, when problems arose, the sales team members considered it Ray's problem, not their own.

After a few short weeks, the products were pulled from the market and Ray was sent packing.

About a year later, Ray's replacement, Morgan took those same product concepts and, giving them a new name, presented them to the sales force for their input. In a few short months, Morgan and his sales force rolled out products that were almost exactly what Ray had tried to introduce. But now, the products were owned by the sales team and Morgan was part of their "us." The new products hit glitches and the sales team members rallied to resolve the problems. The new products were a great success and Morgan stayed on long after I had already moved on to other ventures.

Morgan became one of us, while Ray remained one of them. Ray had not learned one simple thing that every skillful PM knows. Even if you know all the answers, don't give them. Instead, lead the team to discover the answers. That way, you and the team become an "us" to resolve problems.

**Conditioning & Association.** In spite of the admonition to "don't shoot the messenger," if you are associated with bad news, bad events, and unpleasantness, people will be conditioned to dislike you and will not be inclined to help you.

Likewise, the people you associate with will shape the perception others have of you. If you tend to associate with people who are successful, leaders and influencers, then the perceived aura of success and leadership will tend to envelop you as well.

This is true both of the proximate work environment as in your résumé. If you work history is associated with projects that were spectacular failures, you will likely be perceived as a project manager who fails. That will dramatically decrease the value of your professional brand.

When you are engaged in a project and you can see that it is headed toward failure, your first duty is to do all in your power to keep the project from failing. If that effort does not bear fruit, then your second duty is to protect your brand and distance yourself from the failing project.

In the story I mentioned above, Ray engaged me as his program manager. I advised him that he needed to put his ideas in front of the sales leaders and get their participation in the product development. He firmly declined to do that.

I informed Ray that since he was my customer and the customer is always right, that he could do the project the way that he wanted, but he would have to do it with another project manager.

I knew that if I ran the project the way he wanted, it would be a spectacular failure. He ran it his way, and it was every bit as spectacular a failure as I imagined. Only by distancing myself from that project was I able to protect my professional brand. If I had done otherwise, the failure would have likely resulted in my being fired and Ray staying on to try it again, with another PM.

**5) Authority.** Most professional projects managers rarely have any direct (line) authority. We rarely have the power to hire or terminate employees.

Our human resources are provided by various managers and at times we can't even task them directly, without first going through their manager. When it comes to firing a member of the project team, the best we can usually hope for is to get them removed from the project team. At times, we cannot even make that happen.

So, how can a professional project manager, with no formal authority use this principle of influence to get others to do what needs to be done?

The sociologist and philosopher Max Weber in his book *Basic Concepts in Sociology*, distinguishes three types of authority—charismatic, traditional and legal-rational. Most MBA programs note three types of authority as 1) Line, 2) Staff, and 3) Functional authority. Still other sources list five types of authority – Legal, Expert, Reverent, Reward and Punitive.

Legal authority encompasses Line, Staff and Fucntional organizational authorities. And those, likewise tend to encompass both formal Reward and Punitive powers.

Charismatic authority, relying as it does more on the personality and behaviors of the individual, tends to encompass the concepts of expert and reverent authority.

Most PMs, even when they are brought in as contractors or consultants are given no line authority. What we are commonly given is staff authority and some functional authority.

More important than what authority we are given, is what

authority we bring with us, and our knowledge of how to use the authority available to us to the best effect in delivering the project on time, within cost, and with the expected benefits.

The skillful PM always brings a significant degree of expert authority. This must always include expertise in effective project management, and it often includes significant expertise in specific industries or technologies.

Consider what *my LinkedIn profile* says about me. I specialize "in large (>$10mm), high-risk, high-profile projects in the financial services sector." Regardless of this upfront disclaimer, I am often approached with opportunities to manage large construction projects. I ignore those opportunities because that is not my area of greatest strength. Although I am sure I could learn the key ingredients in managing construction projects, I already know some, I don't want to risk my reputation by learning what I don't know about that business at the expense of a client and my reputation as an expert PM.

One tool many project managers use to bolster their expert authority is the earning of the Project Management Professional certification (PMP®) from the Project Management Institute.

This certificate has been aptly compared to an accountant earning their Certified Public Accountant (CPA) certificate.

Like many professional project managers, I have earned my PMP®. After holding it for six years I let mine lapse.

Much like the PMP® or CPA, college degrees also provide evidence of expertise (bolstering the appearance of expert authority).

The MBA is a hallmark of business expertise and opens many doors for those who earn the degree.

I freely confess that I have earned a Bachelors of Computers Sciences, a Masters of Science in Management and a Masters of Science in Project Management for the knowledge they provided me as well as for the credibility (implied expert authority) they give my résumé. Likewise, I have written books (this one included) to educate others as well as to demonstrate and enhance my reputation as an expert in specific topics.

Unfortunately, there are many project managers as well as their potential employers who assume that these paper indicators of expertise assure some basic level of competence and expertise. It is most unfortunate when the project manager himself makes this false assumption.

All those certificates and degrees inferring your expert authority will not save your reputation (or your project) when you undertake large, high-risk, high-profile projects unless you have developed real, significant expertise. That is why my work history also shows my successes in the financial services sector.

The skillful PM comes to the job with real, not just implied, expert authority. The skillful PM knows the difference between the textbook answers and real life.

At best, what a certificate or degree means is that the PM has been taught principles and practices that, when applied correctly, will help strengthen the probability of success for a project. The catch comes in the phrase "applied correctly."

I have seen more than one project manager who religiously followed the practices and used the tools taught while earning their PMP® and were stunned when their projects failed miserably. These paper experts lacked any vestiges of the arts of project management, and usually possessed the mere form, without the real power, of the sciences of project management.

Wisdom, it is said, is the correct application of knowledge. A mere certificate or college degree can never provide assurance that a PM has the wisdom to apply their knowledge correctly. That will only be revealed in the results of your work. And if those don't show up in your résumé, then you are unlikely to ever be taken seriously as a skillful PM.

**6) Scarcity** is perhaps the most widely used and abused tactic for influencing people. It is epitomized in the twin demons of the limited time offer and the limited edition.

It can be a powerful tool for a skillful PM to use when a client lacks the appropriate sense of urgency regarding a project or some key element of the project. But don't ever get caught bluffing with this one, or you will never be believed again (by that client, at least).

Combining scarcity with social proof can significantly increase your power of persuasion.

For instance, if you tell a client that other key industry leaders are already moving forward with this sort of project and when they are fully implemented, they will pull so far ahead of the competition as to be unstoppable, your client is likely to listen closely to what you say next.

If you show him a headline or too that substantiates your claim of industry acceptance and the potential competitive advantage, chances are good that you will get your client's backing.

## CHAPTER 18: NEGOTIATION

"You cannot negotiate with people who say what's mine is mine and what's yours is negotiable."

John F Kennedy

At its most basic level, negotiation is how you get others to do what you want. Everyone has to negotiate. As a skillful project manager, you will use your negotiation skills to get your team to do what you want on a daily basis. At the higher level, you need to use persuasion and negotiation to allow your project to survive the existential threats that come from both internal and external sources. Because not every threat to your project can be persuaded to go away, some will require that you find a way to work around the limitations imposed on you by another project. When that happens, you need to be skilled in the art of negotiation.

*Getting to Yes* by Fisher and Ury is one of the best books on negotiation I have read. The authors address the various approaches to negotiation and boil them down to the only two that really exist: Win-Win and Lose – Lose. The authors then walk you through how to approach negotiations to get what you want.

Every skillful project manager must also become a skilled negotiator. The content of this chapter is largely a "cliffs notes" version of the key concepts presented in *Getting to Yes* and how they are used by skillful project managers. I highly recommend that you make the time to read the original in its complete form.

Because stakeholder involvement is essential for success, and stakeholders are seldom (if ever) amenable to having you dictate to them, you need to negotiate with individuals and groups. Building consensus is a form of negotiation.

In general, there are two broad categories of negotiation, hard and soft. Ury and Fisher proposed a third alternative, which they call "principled negotiation."

Principled negotiation was developed by the Harvard Negotiation Project which sought to establish a merit-based approach to negotiation in place of traditional power or influence based negotiation approaches, typified by hard and soft negotiation tactics.

While hard negotiation tends to be more of a win-lose situation and often results in rancor, both during and after negotiations, it is definitely not the preferred approach for the skillful project manager. In addition, the fact that a project manager is rarely in a position to set down a true "take it or leave it" solution, hard negotiation is often not even an option for the PM.

Soft negotiation is often characterized by a lot of concessions from one side versus the other. It is typically aligned with negotiating either from a position of weakness, or conflict avoidance.

The skillful PM knows that conflict can often be extremely

productive, when managed correctly. This means that conflict avoidance often results in less productivity and inferior results.

Principled negotiation neither actively seeks, nor avoids conflict. Rather it uses conflict creatively, based on principles rather than positions and generally produces results that are far superior to either hard or soft negotiation.

A hallmark of principled negotiation is seeking win-win solutions. This is because of the understanding that win-lose is actually lose-lose. This viewpoint is reinforced by many other sources such as natural law which asserts that we reap what we sow, the law of reciprocity that we give what we get, and the spiritual notion of karma, which suggests that whatever damage or good we do to others ends up being no more nor less than damage or good to ourselves.

Finding ways to create win-win solutions requires more work and imagination, and often more time. Those are the downsides. The upsides are that win-win negotiation tends to require less renegotiation down the road and result in less chances of having the negotiated agreement subsequently overturned. Also, because more creativity is required, the win-win negotiations will often produce a better end-result than would have been achieved with a mandated solution or one achieved based solely on negotiation positions, without regard to principles.

If you look at the problems posed by negotiating peace in the Middle East, you can easily see how the classic positional negotiation impedes any real progress.

Both sides declare that before they will come to the table to discuss peace, certain pre-conditions must be met. Most of the time, these pre-conditions are more posturing and positioning than they are substantive. They are designed to put one side into a position of greater or lesser strength. In traditional negotiation, bargaining power has everything to do with positional power and little or nothing to do with sound principles. And that is why it inevitably falls apart somewhere down the line when the tables are turned and positions are dramatically altered.

Getting to Yes argues that any method of negotiation may be fairly judged by three criteria:

1) It should produce a wise agreement if agreement is possible.
2) It should be efficient. And
3) it should improve or at least not damage the relationship between the parties.

They define a wise agreement as one that
A. meets the legitimate interests of each side to the extent possible,
B. resolves conflicting interests fairly,
C. is durable, and
D. takes community interests into account.)

One of the biggest single problems with positional negotiation is that it ends up becoming a very emotional situation and the egos of the negotiators tend to become intertwined with their positions. Then relinquishing a position is a personal defeat.

This sort of emotional conflict is seldom productive conflict and typically fails to produce wise agreements.

Principled negotiation requires four fundamental actions on the part of the negotiators.
1. **People:** Separate the people from the problem.
2. **Interests:** Focus on interests, not positions.
3. **Options:** Invent multiple options looking for mutual gains before deciding what to do.
4. **Criteria:** Insist that the result be based on some objective standard.

Another key element to principled negotiation is the idea that you are committed to win-win-or-walk-away. This means that if the negotiation is not producing a win-win situation, then you are prepared to walk away from the negotiation.

When Ray wanted to roll out his products without participation from the sales team in the design, I told him that he could do it how he wanted, but he had to do it with another project manager. I was prepared to walk away, even if that meant losing my job.

Ray asked me why I was ready to walk away over this and I told him that I knew that if we went down this road, the program would fail and when it failed his boss would ask me why, laying the failure at my feet. I would end up being shown the door and my reputation would be severely damaged.

Because he recognized my value, Ray offered to indemnify, in writing. Effectively, he put in writing the fact that I advised him to seek the participation of the sales team and he rejected that advice.

I accepted that indemnification. When the program failed, we found ourselves in his boss' office. His boss looked at me and asked why the program failed.

I told him why it failed and he asked me why I let that happen. At this point, true to his word (and without me having to pull out the written evidence) Ray confessed that I advised him and he rejected my advice to take that approach.

The end result was that Ray got fired and my reputation with his boss was firmly established as a project manager who had sound business sense.

Walking away is an extreme action and one that is fraught with peril for you and your client. It is critical that before you play the "walk away" card, you and your client are fully prepared for the consequences of walking away.

In some cases, it may not be possible for your client to walk away. In those cases, you and your client need to decide in advance if you can abide by the worst possible outcome of the negotiations.

However, if your opponent is committed to principled negotiation, the likelihood of having to walk away is dramatically decreased, since they are also seeking a win-win solution.

When negotiation is called for, the skillful PM doesn't just leap into negotiation mode. Rather, you need to analyze the four elements above as they relate to the situation and see them both from your own perspective as well as from that of the other party (or parties). Then, you need to develop your alternatives and plan your negotiation.

Although this may sound Machiavellian, it is not. Your analysis identifies obstacles and solutions, your planning determines how to present those obstacles and solutions/alternatives in ways that don't alienate or offend your counterparts on the other side of the table. The skillful PM knows well that presentation is paramount. <u>How</u> you say something can be even more important than _what_ you say.

During the actual negotiation discussions, it is usually helpful to use the four elements noted above as the framework for your discussions.

If you and those you negotiate with can agree in advance to embrace and follow the principles and practices of principled negotiation, then your probability for achieving wise agreements are almost guaranteed.

Unfortunately, not all negotiations and negotiators are prepared in advance with these principles and practices. The skillful project manager, when confronted with positional negotiations will pause to educate and seek to change the rules of the game from positional to principled negotiation.

If, in spite of your encouragement and education, your opponent refuses to move away from positional negotiation into principled negotiation, you will very likely have to provide a brief, action-based education in the reality of your commitment to win-win-or-walk-away.

A final note is in order on the walk-away. Walking away today, does not mean that you refuse to come back to the negotiation. It may mean that you are enforcing a pause in the negotiation so that all parties can do more research and return to the negotiation with better solutions. Walking away is a legitimate form of conflict and conflict management. It is especially useful to recalibrate a conflict or negotiation to produce more productive outcomes.

## CHAPTER 19: MEASUREMENT

"What gets measured, gets improved."
Peter Drucker

Measurement, on its face, may smack of the science of project management. However, this section is not about how to define measurements and carry them out. That is science. Rather, this section is about what you should, and should not be measuring.

You should be measuring results. You should not be worrying about measuring activity.

Many of the tools and processes used in the science of project management are easily diverted into tracking activity instead of delivering results. The ability to consistently and effectively differentiate between activity and results that separates the project management scientist from the skillful project manager.

Experienced project managers have dealt with circumstances

where project tasks attained the 99% complete mark, but were never completed. This is the classic example of activity versus results. Even such wonderful progress management tools such as Earned Value Analysis (EVA) can end up measuring activity instead of results.

As a PM I always make it a habit to focus on results instead of activity. I am much less interested in knowing how many hours were logged toward completing a deliverable. I am very keenly interested in knowing if the deliverable will be produced and completed by the projected date. If a deliverable is late, I may be interested to know if the effort toward its completion is above or below the budget. But that is only valuable information to me in the perspective of the prospective delivery date.

Using PM tools to constantly present management with activity reports is little more than a shell game, or smoke and mirrors to keep the client distracted from the lack of actual results. It plays out this way too in the big picture of project management.

Too often the purpose, the desired result, of a project gets lost or ignored along the way. The purpose of the project becomes to move through the project life cycle from beginning to end. But, if the project doesn't yield the desired business results, then it is a failure, even if all the project management processes were executed flawlessly and on time.

I began my path in this business as a computer programmer and systems analyst. Too often in that experience, we delivered a program that met all the stated business requirements, but it didn't do the job that the business needed done. It didn't actually solve their problem. That was most often the result of the failure to clearly articulate and understand the problem and to continually refer back to the problem to evaluate progress toward the solution.

Defense contracting solutions for large weapon systems are almost synonymous with cost overruns. These overruns happen consistently, and in spite of extensive requirements for detailed estimations and tracking of work.

In a typical, large defense contract a project management office (PMO) is staffed with dozens of people whose sole jobs are to track the work being done compared to the schedule of work which has been devised as the plan to deliver the weapon system.

Every day, or week, people working on the project record the time they have worked and align those hours worked to specific project tasks.

Each project task has been carefully estimated to consume a certain amount of labor in order to deliver a specific deliverable which in needed to complete the larger project.

In spite of all the math and science used, many of the tasks use up all the hours assigned to get the work done and the deliverable is still not ready for the next stage of work.

The processes and tools to estimate and track labor in project work are extremely extensive and well thought out. They have also proven to be almost entirely ineffective in delivering tangible, high-quality results which meet the client needs within budget and schedule constraints.

Without going into all the details of trying to solve this massive problem, I will simply say that the extensive estimation and tracking is part of the problem, not part of the solution, because they are all aimed at measuring and tracking activity (labor hours delivered) instead of focusing on results.

In most large corporations the need for maintaining a group of competent project managers and business analysts available for use on an ever-changing portfolio of problems leads to the creation of a Project Management Office (PMO).

Within each PMO the manager needs ways to measure and rate the abilities of the individual project managers and to assure that all projects are delivered with a uniformly high quality and maintainability.

One way this is typically achieved is through the application of PMO Standards. These standards most often are comprised of standard checklists of documents which each PM is supposed to produce during the lifecycle of each project. Each document has a standard template, the uniformity making it easier for managers to find what they want to focus on regardless of the writing or communications skills of each PM or business analyst (BA).

To figure out what activities are needed to produce each of these management deliverables, members of the PMO are often required to learn or become certified as Project Management Professionals and to become well acquainted with the Project

# The Art of Project Management

Management Body of Knowledge (PMBOK®) which the Project Management Institute promotes as the "Bible" for the discipline (religion) of project management.

As I noted early on in this book, the PMBOK® and its related studies are all about the science of project management.

All this focus on checklists and standard project management documents often means that the skill and value of the project managers is judged by how brilliantly they can complete the project management documents within the standards required by their PMO overseers.

Unfortunately, all these PMO checklists and documents are all about the activities of project management and not at all about the actual results of the project management and about the actual results of the project.

While the PMO is focused on ensuring that the PM has checked off that business requirements have been documented and accepted by management, the project manager is often so busy checking the boxes that s/he neither knows, nor cares, that the requirements themselves are incomplete, inadequate, poorly written, and unverifiable.

Being able to ask the right questions of the right people about the contents of those business requirements and having the savvy to recognize that the attitudes and answers of the business experts often reveals more about the completeness and verifiability of those requirements than you can read in the pages of the documents is where the skillful PM is separated from the merely competent one.

The skillful PM is able to discern the difference between measuring activity and measuring results and focuses on results.

I worked as a contracted PM on a very large project where data migration from a legacy system to a new system played a key role. Where the corporate PMO was focused on ensuring I completed checklists and project management documents, I was focused on making sure that the legacy data model and the future state data model were reconciled through the extraction, transformation and loading programs and through the key regulatory and financial management reports data elements. I wanted to be sure that when the system was implemented, the key business tools used to monitor the health of their company were at least as effective, accurate and robust in the new system as they were in the old.

I could have simply met the PMO demands and they would have deemed me "competent." They might have even maintained that assessment and ascribed any subsequent project failure to outside circumstances. However, I know enough to not let measurements of activity distract from measurements of results. Not only did I meet their PMO demands, but I implemented and employed my own measures to improve and measure the processes I had to build so that I would fully understand and be able to articulate the results of my efforts to migrate their data.

The data checks I designed were put in place and ensured that the data migration maps were not only fully documented, but they were compared against all the downstream processes and reports to ensure that all the necessary data was being migrated. They went on to ensure that all the records that should be moved were, and that each record was moved without being corrupted and that legacy data cleanliness issues were not pushed into the new system, but were instead resolved before or during migration. Delivering complete, accurate, correct, and quality data allowed others to focus on ensuring that the processing of the data was completed as expected, instead of letting data migration and data quality problems distract them from the functionality of the system.

> **"There is nothing quite so useless as doing with great efficiency something that should not be done at all."**
> 
> Peter Drucker

The Art of Project Management

© Copyright 2017 by @ kbuntu, Image used with permission through DepositPhotos.com

## CHAPTER 20: TECHNICAL SKILLS

"A man's got to know his limitations."
Clint Eastwood
as Detective (Dirty) Harry Callahan
Magnum Force, 1973

The skillful project manager will always have skills that fall in the category of technical skills. This is typically embodied in having skills with several pieces of office productivity software that are common for most offices and some which are specific to project managers.

The skillful project manager is familiar with more than one project management tool as well as being comfortable with using and building spread sheets, position papers, and creating effective presentations using tools like MS Power Point.

**Area(s) of Expertise** – Although the principles of project management are universal, their application in different industries present different challenges.

My background is based in computer programming, defense contracting and financial services. Although I have managed multi-million dollar, enterprise-wide projects for one of the top 10 banks in the US, when I get job leads on construction projects, I pass them by. I don't consider them because I know enough about construction work to understand that I know far too little about it to walk in the door and start delivering quality results. Instead, I would require a steep learning curve, and would very likely be ignorant of significant risks and issues that are inherent in all construction projects.

When I take on a project, I want to be able to readily justify the rate I am being paid. Although I could use "smoke and mirrors", bravado and daunting presentations to succeed at convincing my client I am worth my pay for a time. If I don't actually know what I am doing and understand how to manage the project effectively, eventually I will be found out. And, when my smoke and mirrors are seen through, my reputation as a project manager will take a hit. My brand will be damaged. Perhaps, it will be damaged beyond repair.

Because I value my reputation, my brand, as a project manager and a professional, I limit my project management engagements to areas where I have a decent understanding. Because I am an incorrigible life-long learner, I am continually educating myself in new areas and in greater depth within the areas I already know. Regardless of this expanding knowledge base, I offer full disclosure to any prospective client who wants me to take on work that is outside of my primary areas of expertise.

A project manager who believes that project management is project management no matter what industry you are in, is a project manager who lacks sufficient experience and is headed for at least one very expensive failure.

The Skillful PM knows s/he should play to strengths whenever possible. You cannot do that very well when you don't have sufficient understanding of the industry which is the context for the project. When you find yourself in totally unfamiliar ground, you will become too dependent upon the subject matter experts (SMEs) around you. If they are both trustworthy as well as knowledgeable, you may succeed. But, if they have their own axes to grind, you could find your head on the chopping block.

**Contracts** – A skillful project manager must have at least a basic understanding of business law is required for most project managers. Not all project management roles require you to deal directly with vendors, but when they do, you need to read and understand the contracts that have been established, as well as having the knowledge to negotiate contracts as needed. Ultimately, contracts should not be signed until proper legal review has been completed, but the lawyers also need your business perspective to ensure the contract delivers what you need.

Another reason the skillful PM needs to understand contracts and business law is to understand and identify legal risks which can devastate an otherwise successful project.

If you don't understand what legal liabilities your project can trigger with clients, customers, and team members, then you are very likely going to find your project going down in flames and a lot of your time spent giving legal depositions. Neither of those are fun prospects.

All that being said, when it comes to writing contracts, I leave that the business attorneys. They are trained in writing things in legalese so that it is binding in court. However, the Skillful Pm won't leave them to their own devices.

The Skillful PM manages the contract lawyers much like any other sub-team, giving them clear requirements for what is needed and reviewing the content of their deliverables carefully to ensure that the needs of the project are being met by what the contracts require, reward, and punish.

**Team Building** – Building a real team, not just recruiting a bunch of individuals is an essential skill for successful project managers. Because team building involves relationship building skills and leadership skills, this falls into the "art" portion of project management skills.

Hiring friends to be on your team is usually not a good idea. Keep friends for friendship, but work with the skilled and competent, whether you like them or not. Even be willing to hire your enemies, if they are the most competent and skilled people you can find.

Too often, when you hire friends, they presume on your friendship and put you in difficult positions which undermine your leadership and may force you to choose between doing what you should and losing a friend. When you are leading, you can be friendly and caring, but you cannot be friends with those you lead. You must be a good leader first, and a good friend second. If your friends cannot or will not understand and respect that, then they will not serve you well as team members.

When you assemble an highly skilled team, your probability of having an high performing team is dramatically increased. And the high performing team will deliver extraordinary results which will propel you to success. To this end, when you are hiring or recruiting team members, never accept the best of the worst. If a prospective team member does not meet or exceed your minimum needs for the role, then move on. If you interview an hundred people and none are qualified, then empty out the candidate pool and keep looking. If you take a shortcut and hire the best candidate out of a group where none of them qualify, you will regret it. The time or money you save by hiring an unqualified candidate will be more than expended to make up for the deficiencies and problems required by the substandard performance you get from under-qualified team members.

A key piece of team building is for your team members to get to know and trust each other. If your team is distributed, this is a bit harder to pull off and requires some very deliberate effort on your part.

When a team is co-located, they will tend to have hallway and break room chats as well as conversations before and after meetings. These casual conversations usually provide opportunities for team members to build relationships of respect and trust.

Even with these opportunities for ad hoc familiarization of team members, the skillful project manager will deliberately arrange and encourage opportunities for team members to establish solid bonds with each other. The marketplace is replete with team building ideas. Find some that you're are comfortable with and use them judiciously.

When your team is geographically distributed, team building is more difficult and requires a greater amount of thoughtful effort by a skillful project manager.

The first key to knitting together a group of individuals into a team is that each member of the team needs to become "real" to the other members of the team. If a team member remains nothing more than a disembodied voice on conference calls, or emails, they will not be tightly integrated into the fabric of the team.

A low-tech answer to this is to have current photos and resumes, short biographic sketches or CVs of each team member posted on a team site where they are visible to all members of the team. Being able to put a face with a voice helps make the team member to be more of a real person to other team members. Adding information on their experience and qualifications to that allows team members to have a context for comments and questions coming from that team member.

Adding the occasional, or even regular, video conference to the mix allows team members to gain a more nuanced feel for their distant team members. Reading body language and expressions conveys many subtle messages which help to build a team that respects and trusts each other.

Getting your team members together for one or two days of face-to-face interactions is highly recommended, and it will significantly shorten the time it takes for a team to become a properly functioning unit.

Regardless of whether your team is co-located, distributed, or a combination of both, they will still go through the normal stages of team building: Forming, Norming, Storming and Performing. When geography separates your team members from you and from each other, your challenge in moving your team through these stages is significantly exacerbated.

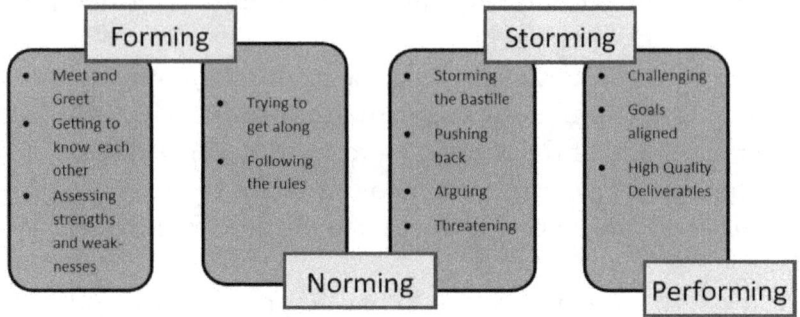

While some change the order of Norming and Storming, my experience has been that after the initial team formation, people go through a period where they are trying to be good "corporate citizens" and they "go-along to get along," until they finally get fed up and explode into a storm of fighting and issues. This can be a great period of creative conflict.

I was working with a team that was comprised of contractors, full-time employees and employees from a vendor. The vendor was trying to "gently" force the team to conform to their process model for requirements gathering.

Early during the third all-day team meeting I had to leave the meeting for an hour. When I returned, I found that all the members of the vendor team were gone from the room. I asked the people who remained if they were on a break.

They replied that they had strongly invited the vendor team to leave and not come back until they had a better way of doing things.

I had been waiting for this moment from the very first day. I had recognized that the vendor's approach was deeply flawed and that the employees and contractors were skeptical.

Regardless of their skepticism, they had "participated" in more than sixteen hours of work before finally getting fed up and losing their cool with an approach that they could feel in their bones was not going work to get what everyone needed.

My only dismay was that they had wasted so much time forming and norming before they hit the storming. Knowing the group, and the flaws of the vendor's process, I had hoped for the blowup. I knew that only an extreme, adverse reaction would be sufficient to convince the vendor to set their process aside and adopt one more suited to the reality of this situation.

I immediately set to work, talking with the folks in the room, I had them start listing on the board what was wrong with the vendor's approach and why it wouldn't work. After they vented for about 20 minutes, I shifted the focus and asked them what about the vendor's approach was working well, and why. Next, I moved them on to how things could be done differently that would achieve the desired results. About then, the leader of the vendor team ushered his people back into the room.

I explained why the team had exploded, what they felt was wrong about the process. I then moved on to what was right about the process. Finally, I engaged both the vendor and the employee / contractor team to describe what could be done to achieve the results we needed.

After that storm, the team began to perform, very well. They had a process which was agreed upon by all. They felt that their objections had been heard and acted upon, and they felt a mutual respect for each other and the emotional, not just rational, realization that everyone was operating toward the same end and in good faith.

In spite of how some might consider team building an art, because of its similarity to relationship management, I consider it a technical or scientific skill. I put it in that category because group dynamics are much more predictable than those of individuals by themselves.

Team building is about a lot of group dynamics. There is a significant element of peer pressure involved and getting the Alphas in the room to believe they are actually running things. Then the Betas feel they are following the Alphas, who they know, instead of this project management stranger who has been thrust upon them.

## CHAPTER 21: BRAND MANAGEMENT

*"All of us need to understand the importance of branding. We are CEOs of our own companies: Me Inc."*

Tom Peters in Fast Company

As a professional PM your reputation and your brand will make a significant difference in the rates you can charge for your services and the kinds of projects that will come your way. You must be aware of your brand and manage your brand. It exists whether or not you realize its presence. Failing to manage your brand is failing to manage your career.

Your reputation and your brand are inextricable. Anything which depreciates your reputation has a corresponding impact on your brand.

Your brand is both about what you do, and how you do it. A

solid brand reputation will usually mean it is easier for you to put money in the bank doing what you like to do.

As an example, imagine that you could buy one of two cars from me. One is a Mercedes Benz 600 Series and the other is a car I built myself in my garage. Each will cost you $60,000. Knowing only what you know now, which would you buy?

Even if I assure you that my car has been built with such innovative technology that it never needs maintenance and will run for an hundred miles on a single gallon of fuel. You are still unlikely to be swayed to buy my home built special.

However, if three of your most trusted friends have all bought home built cars from me and they all swear that they are the next best things to owning the flying DeLorean from the movie <u>Back to the Future</u>, you might very well find yourself handing over your $60,000 to me and taking my no-name car home to your garage.

The difference is what results when a brand is trusted and has a good reputation.

The value of a brand is not all about price, but it does impact what you and I are willing to pay for an item and where we go looking for it. When you go shopping at WalMart, you expect to find reasonable quality products at a low price. When you go shopping at Nordstroms, you expect to find only very high quality items and the price, even on sale, will likely always be higher than any comparable item you might buy at WalMart.

This variance in price and quality doesn't mean you won't go shopping at WalMart, it simply frames your expectations for what you will find.

When Sears bought K-Mart one thing they tried to do was to dress up the interiors and displays in K-Mart stores to look a bit more upscale like a Sears store. They even brought in brand name lines such as Martha Stewart and Jaclyn Smith. The efforts didn't lift sales. K-Mart buyers were looking for serviceable clothing at low prices. The upscale images were out of place in a store made famous by its "blue light specials," unadvertised spot sales.

Your brand needs to be shaped to align with not only the value you can deliver, but with the mindset of the clients you hope to attract. You need to consider both your actions, and the engagements you take on in the light of the brand you want to embody.

You can find courses and books devoted wholly to the topics of marketing and managing your brand. They will explain how to use social media and other avenues to put your brand identity in front of your target audience.

However, while learning how to promote your brand, don't lose sight of the essential reality of what you can and cannot deliver. Because your brand is one of your biggest assets when seeking a project management engagement, you need to be aware of what you truly can and cannot do well. A fearless and utterly candid self-assessment is the first step. However, it is not enough.

In addition to your self-assessment, I suggest you seek out project managers who are currently managing projects that are much larger than what you have ever before managed. Find a way to get time with them. Pay them for their time if you must.

Then, ask them to help you honestly and thoroughly evaluate your skills and abilities. Be prepared to hear things about you that won't be complimentary. Don't get defensive or attempt to explain things away. Accept the input, examine it in detail and then ask your mentor what you can do to improve your skills and up your game to the level you want to attain.

Many of the project managers I have interviewed for roles in large projects have sincerely believed they knew how to manage large projects, even though they lacked experience.

Many of them hadn't a clue of the real and potentially devastating differences between the level of skills needed for managing a $500k project versus and $5mm project versus a $15mm project.

During the same time I was hiring experienced, proven project managers, others around me were hiring project managers who had great potential or talked a good talk.

Those project managers with positive potential all ended up being chewed up and spit out by the very large project I was hiring for. To be perfectly honest, even a few of the proven, experienced PMs got chewed up and spit out. However, in contrast to the potential performers, the proven, experienced PMs didn't leave behind them a wake of chaos and damage to the project which I then had to fix, or hire someone to fix.

## The Art of Project Management

If you want to avoid earning a reputation as a PM who bit off more than they could chew, you need to understand the difference between the art and the science of project management, and you need to become expert at both – or dial back your career expectations to roles that are on the right level for your skills.

© Copyright 2017 by @ ivelin, Image used with permission through DepositPhotos.com

## CHAPTER 22: THE WRONG PM FOR THE JOB

*"The end is never the end. It's always the beginning of something."*

Kate Lord Brown
The Perfume Garden

Truly skillful project managers who can properly manage large, high-risk, high-profile projects are not as plentiful as folks would like to think. Many companies maintain a Project Management Office (PMO) stocked with skilled PMs who have been indoctrinated in the methods the company prefers to use. Many of them have (or are required to earn) a PMP®, further reinforcing the image of knowledgeable authority and skill which they possess.

When a large project comes along, the business leaders typically look to their PMO to provide the right talent. Unfortunately, most PMOs don't have anyone with experience at the level needed, because those large projects don't come along very often. Too often, the leader of the PMO either doesn't realize the gap in skills between what is on hand and what is needed, or s/he fears it will reflect badly on their own performance to tell the Board of Directors that outside talent is going to be needed to manage this kind of effort.

This situation sets the organization up for failure, because no one, not the PMO, not the PMs, and certainly not the business sponsor know what they don't know about managing these kind of large, enterprise-wide endeavors.

Because of this, the in-house PMO tends to provide corporate leadership with a false sense of security regarding the organization capacity to take on large (balance-sheet impacting) projects. Failure to have a PM with the appropriate level of successful experience at this level is a critical error that will almost certainly cost millions of dollars.

This is a real problem which has cost more than one company tens and hundreds of millions of dollars. It is not a "might-be" or hypothetical issue.

> **"a little ditty about Jack and Dianne, two American kids doing the best that they can."**
> The Ballad of Jack and Diane
> John Cougar-Mellencamp

A few years ago, I had the experience of being brought on to manage a portion (worth about $30mm) of a much larger program with a financial services company. In this program I had a front-row seat watching the exact scenario I describe above.

One of the lead program managers, overseeing about a third of the scope of the program, was a home-grown PM from the corporate PMO. While Jack (not the real name) had proven to be an excellent project manager up to this point, the very skills that made him a good PM were the same which made him a lousy program manager.

Having never previously managed such a large effort, Jack attacked the job in the same ways that always worked before.

He got deep into the details and worked hard to bring every aspect of the work under his personal scrutiny and control.

Because Jack was so far down in the weeds, he wasn't looking at the big picture. He didn't see several threats and issues coming until they were already adversely impacting the program. Because of that inattention (which was repeated time and again), the program experienced one delay after another, costing tens of millions of unexpected expenses.

Although Jack remained at the helm, his efforts were augmented by a raft off additional PMs, specialists and business analysts who were able to work through the problems and deliver the program more than a year late and with a significantly larger budget (by many tens of millions of dollars) than was originally planned.

In contrast with Jack, the same company hired Dianne, a seasoned Senior Enterprise Project Manager who had experience with successfully delivering large programs like this, to handle the other major part of this same program, as a peer to Jack.

Dianne started right away by hiring project managers from outside the company onto her team. She sought out PMs who had successful experience delivering large, high-risk, high-profile projects.

She expected her PMs to dig deep into the details in their areas and to properly manage the work, issues and risks in their own respective realms. Meanwhile, she was busy looking at the big picture (and when her PMs failed to perform, she fired them and brought in others to do the job until she established a very high-performing team).

So foresaw and surfaced interdependencies between bodies of work. She applied industry best practices instead of accepting that "we have always done it this way." Her actions gave the Board of Directors timely advance notice of both realistic (though aggressive) timelines and what it would take in terms of people, budget, and other resources to get the job done.

When Jack's part of the program faltered and didn't look like it would survive, the Board of Directors called in an outside firm to look at the entire effort and determine if it could or should be continued.

In Jack's program they found a significant level of disarray and inefficiency. Jack's need for control and focus on minute details created bottlenecks and unnecessary dependencies. His home-grown approach resulted in processes that were deeply flawed and often ineffective.

The outside consultants prescribed some dramatic changes in how the work was being managed and inserted themselves into an oversight role to help mitigate the risks. This was another expensive and unplanned addition to the budget.

They separated Jack's area of responsibility into two parts, leaving him to push across the finish line the subset of work that was nearest to completion and took over the direct management of the remainder of Jack's work, frantically restructuring the team and its processes to enable it to deliver as planned.

After delivering their assessment and recommendations regarding Jack's portion of the program, they turned their attention to Dianne's efforts, expecting to find a similar situation (and opportunity for fee income for them).

To their surprise, they found that Dianne's portion of the work was on time, in spite of an aggressive schedule and several resource challenges. Dianne and her team were already applying industry best practices and had used failures in Jack's program as the lever to introduce lessons learned to drive organizational acceptance of many of these best practices. In fact, the outside company found almost no opportunity in Dianne's area to insert themselves because whatever best practices they had hoped to bring to the table were already in place within Dianne's team.

Unfortunately, in living proof of the axiom that "no good deed goes unpunished," management decided that Dianne's work needed to be slowed down to that Jack's late deliveries could be properly absorbed by the organization before Dianne's could be brought on line.

Although I have changed the names, the story of Jack and Dianne is a true one. It played out just as I have described it. In the end, the one-third of the program scope that was originally in Jack's area of responsibility will cost the company almost the same amount they will pay to deliver the two-thirds which Dianne is prepared to deliver.

Fortunately for the client, the extreme measures taken to salvage the work in Jack's areas paid off and allowed the successful implementation of the first part of the program. The second portion, which was taken out of Jack's control is moving forward on track and will decreasing levels of risk across the board. I have no doubt that when the Board of Directors reinvigorate Dianne's portion of the program (if she or someone with her qualifications is at the helm), it will go quickly and without major surprises.

When I began this book, it was in the hope that I could achieve something meaningful and helpful for my fellow project managers and their clients. Very selfishly, I also hoped it would reduce the number of times in the future when I find myself interviewing a project manager to help me on a large, high-risk, high-profile project, only to find I have wasted my time (and theirs) because they haven't the slightest clue of what it takes to run a truly large, enterprise-wide project.

By noting in this book both the difference between the art and science of project management as well as giving some instruction in the former, I hope I will help aspiring project managers to see beyond earning a certification or degree to build a learning plan that will help them to become a truly skillful PM.

And, it does take a learning plan. You are unlikely to acquire the kind of knowledge you need to become truly skillful unless you have the wit and will to methodically learn and practice you skills, seeking opportunities to both reveal and close the gaps in your skills set.

If you think there is some essential art of project management I have left off my list here, I invite you to let me know your thoughts. Perhaps you will point out something I overlooked, and you may be a co-author with me on a subsequent edition of this book.

If, as you read these chapters, you said to yourself (or others), "he isn't telling the whole story. There is a whole lot more to this skill than what Tom says in this book," I will say, I couldn't agree more. This is just one book. I don't pretend it contains all you need to know or do. Rather, it points you toward the topics you need to study and research in greater depth and learn to master them.

© Copyright 2017 by @ Mind-Map, Image used with permission through DepositPhotos.com

## CHAPTER 23: APPLYING THE 80/20 RULE

"Education is learning what you didn't even know you didn't know."

Daniel Boorstin, SJD

After reading all this, to move ahead, you need to apply the 80/20 rule to the art of project management.

The 80/20 rule, also known as a Pareto Principle, or the law of the vital few states that in many cases you get 80% of your effects from 20% of your actions. Joseph Juran, One of the founders of the total quality management (aka Six Sigma) movement named this principle after the Italian economist Vilfredo Pareto who noted the connection in a paper he published in 1896.

Experience, both my own and that of many others, suggests

that the Pareto Principle seems to be amazingly universal in its application. It occurs both in nature and in the world of finance. Banks make 80% of their revenues from 20% of their customers. Salesmen make 80% of their commissions from 20% of their customers. Software engineers know that if they fix the top 20% of defects, they will eliminate 80% of reported errors. Occupational safety experts know that fixing the right 20% of hazards will eliminate 80% of the injuries. I could go on, but I won't.

The reality of project management is that the art of project management is the 20% of project management that gets you 80% of the results. And within the art of project management, there is a 20% that will yield 80% of the results.

In this chapter, I will tell you the 20% of the 20% that has given me 80% of my results.

#1 Know Thyself
#2 Be the Leader You Want
#3 Manage Your Own Stress

## 1) KNOW THYSELF

**"The first thing you have to know is yourself. A man who knows himself can step outside himself and watch his own reactions like an observer."**
Adam Smith, The Money Game

In the Greek temple of Apollo the phrase "know thyself" was etched into the wall and taught as a truth and skill required in order to come to understand the gods. The phrase is reputed to have been adopted by the Greeks from their Egyptian mentors from before the days of Socrates and Plato. Plato, however, made it most famous by its use in his writings about Socrates.
It is the single most valuable piece of advice you will likely ever receive.

Knowing yourself requires that you conduct a fearless self-assessment. This exercise will identify and validate both your strengths and your weaknesses. It will help you to begin to realize the full extent of what you know and what you don't know. Perhaps the most important knowledge to gain from this exercise is to expand your self-awareness so that you become aware of what you don't know. When you know what you don't know, you realize the danger of taking on work in a space where your ignorance is unbounded.

You can use the table of contents of this book as a guide to your own fearless self-assessment, or you can use the shorter version provided in the next section.

## Five Key Areas for Self Assessment

I have identified five key areas for fearless self-assessments as project managers. In each of these areas, you should rate yourself on a scale of 1 to 10 where 1 is you are a novice and 10 is you are an expert.

1. Communications skills
2. Interpersonal skills
3. Leadership skills
4. Adaptability
5. Work Values

**Communication skills** – How good a communicator are you? The first skill you need to master to be a good communicator is to learn how to listen.

I recall interviewing a job candidate and asking, "what is the single most important skill they could bring to the table as a project manager?" The answer, "Communication. Communication, attention to detail, and persistence."

If the candidate had actually been a good communicator, he would have realized that listening is the most important part of communication, and he would have listened when I asked him to name the single most important skill, and listed only one skill, not three. He didn't get the job.

In addition to rating yourself as a listener, rate your abilities with both the written and spoken word.

**Interpersonal skills** – How easily do you connect with other people and establish positive, working relationships with them? Are you good at persuasion and negotiation? How good are you at persuading, negotiating and establishing rapport one-on-one and with a group?

**Leadership skills** – Rate how well you can motivate others. How are your team-building skills and delegation?

**Adaptability** – How good are you at "rolling with the punches," "changing gears quickly," and adjusting plans to meet new situations? How creative are you with problem solving? How good are you at learning quickly? Rate yourself on your ability to adjust priorities.

**Work Values** – How dependable are you? How honest are you? How confident are you? How positive is your attitude in the face of obstacles? How committed are you to your endeavors? How persistent?

Performing a fearless self-assessment in these five areas will help you to identify areas of strength and areas for improvement.

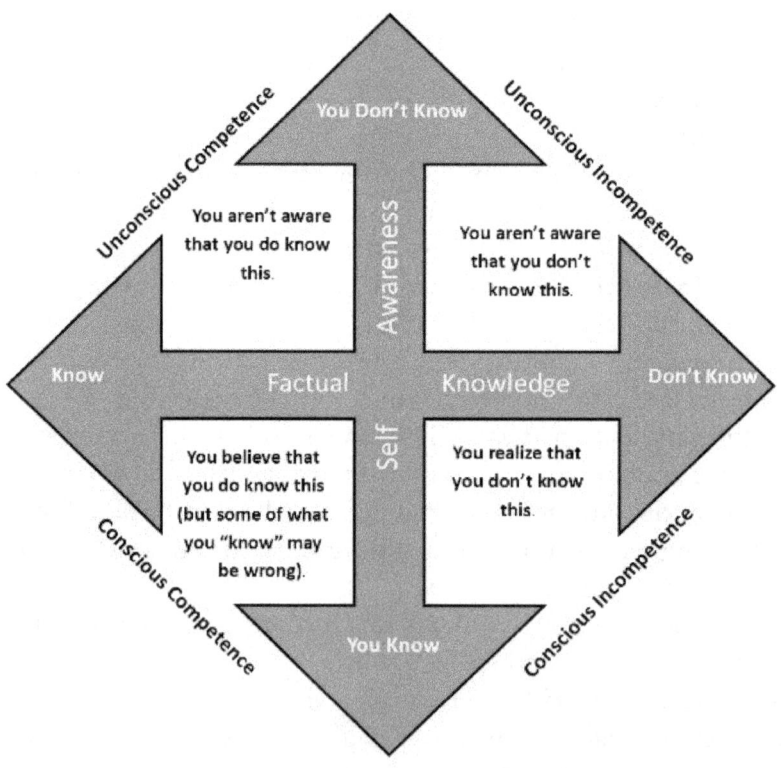

© 2017 by A+ Results, LLC, Used with Permission

When **you don't know what you don't know**, you are in a state of ignorance that can hurt you badly. You are unconsciously incompetent. You don't even know enough to know when you are doing a very bad job.

When you invest your resources or those of a company in an area where you don't know what you don't know, you are gambling. Taking on a project management role in this space will ensure that you have a lot of failures to learn from. Hiring a project manager who is unaware of what s/he doesn't know, is a sure way to have cost and schedule overruns, and potentially catastrophic failure for your project.

When **you know what you don't know**, you have managed to put some boundaries on your ignorance. Now, you are consciously incompetent. As insulting as that sounds, it is a good thing.

Being aware of your shortcomings allows you to use those boundaries to your advantage. Not knowing those boundaries versus being aware of them makes the difference, respectively, between gambling and taking calculated risks. Taking on a project in this space is risky. However, because of your awareness of your ignorance, you can effectively use risk management strategies. You can hire expertise in the area to reduce the risk, or you can outsource that work to shift the risk.

A second major benefit of a fearless self-assessment is that you might well discover that you become aware that you know more than you were aware that you knew. If **you don't know what you know,** you are unconsciously competent. I had this happen in my real estate investing several years ago.

I had been investing for several years and worked hard to educate myself in this space. I was attending a three-day seminar from a leading industry expert and chatting with some fellow attendees. As we discussed the topics, I found myself explaining concepts and practices the speaker had touched on to my fellow attendees. Several of them remarked that I could have taught the entire seminar myself. At that moment, I realized they were right. I knew more than I realized. I had internalized and used the knowledge to the point where it had become unconscious competence. And with that realization, my self-awareness boundary shifted and I became consciously competent in that space.

When **you know what you know,** you are consciously competent. However, there is a danger in this space. The danger comes when you think you know, but you don't actually know because what you "know" is wrong.

The keys to changing your competence are fearless self-assessments and a commitment to life-long learning.

**Life-long Learning.** Be willing to learn from anyone. Take classes. Read books. Seek out experts. Seek out the successful and the unsuccessful. Learn from the failures and successes of others. They have paid the tuition and taken the test. With some effort on your part you can get the "A" grade by taking the test without having had to go through the entire experience for yourself.

Write a book. Pick a subject you want to learn about. Grab a notebook and start listing why you want to know and what you want to know. Then, start doing research (see the paragraph above). Take notes. From time to time, go through your research and write down the key learnings you have discovered. You may ultimately publish this book, or you may just use it as a learning journal to capture and clarify your knowledge of a subject.

# 2) BE THE LEADER YOU WANT

> **"Be the change you want to see in others."**
> Mahatma Gandhi

Elsewhere in this book I mention one of the great natural laws, the Law of the Harvest. When it comes to being a leader understanding the application of this law is essential. You reap what you sow. You become what you do.

Throughout your life you will find yourself under the leadership of a variety of individuals. Their styles will inspire you, either to follow them or to run from them. While you are either running toward or away from these putative leaders, take the time to study them. Identify why their leadership makes you want to follow or flee.

As you identify what makes a good and bad leader, do your own fearless self-assessment and determine what you need to learn to do, or to stop doing, to become the kind of leader you like to follow. Then, begin applying that learning in your life.

Learn how to lead from the middle, before you try to lead from the front.

Learn how to lead volunteers, as well as conscripts. Almost anyone can get people to do what they want under the threat of job-loss. Getting volunteers to consistently do what you want, and have them coming back for more, requires real leadership ability.

In my own life, I have been privileged to have a variety of leadership experiences which have shaped my abilities. As a missionary for the Church of Jesus Christ of Latter-day Saints (aka the Mormon Church), I was challenged to lead a small team of volunteers in a foreign country. As part of that effort, I had to learn how to lead church members as well. Later, as a Marine NCO, I was given formal leadership instruction and opportunities to lead other Marines.

Beyond the Marine Corps, I learned to lead from the middle and the front as I worked my way up through corporate management hierarchies. Along the way, I stayed involved in volunteer organizations. I joined Toastmasters and received additional formal and informal leadership training and practice leading volunteers who could walk away at a moment's notice without any repercussions.

My experience as a project manager has been primarily in roles where I held little or no organizational authority. In these roles I have led project teams spanning every organizational silo whose total membership included hundreds of individuals and managers with organizational positions both below and above my own organizational 'rank.' Regardless, it was my privilege and responsibility to build them into an high-performing team and lead them to deliver exceptional results for our client/employer.

Some leaders have a reputation for being ruthless. Others are extremely kind and caring. Some are autocratic, others have a participatory approach to making decisions. For every leadership style that exists you can find notable examples of both success and failure. Notice that I don't tell you what sort of leader you should be. Rather, I tell you to be the kind of leader you want.

I say that because whatever type of leader you want, will lead you to the organization that thrives with that sort of leader. My own leadership approach is a balancing act of accomplishing the mission and taking care of people. It doesn't fit with all organizations. That doesn't bother me at all. Finding out what kind of organization I am dealing with is an essential part of my due diligence when considering taking on a project management role.

In 280 and 279 BC King Pyrrhus of Epirus defeated the legions of the Roman Empire in the battles of Heraclea and Asculum. Unfortunately, in gaining the victories Pyrrhus suffered the loss of almost all of his principal commanders, people he could not readily replace. When congratulated on his victories he replied, "Another such victory and I come back to Epirus alone." This sort of self-destructive victory was named a Pyrrhic Victory in honor of the victories of King Pyrrhus over the Romans.

If I can achieve the mission without putting extreme stress on my team, I will do that. If achieving the mission requires that I sacrifice the well-being of my team members, I will do that if I feel that that the value of the objective outweighs the damage to be done. I do want to be the winner of any Pyrrhic victories.

When working in the insurance division of a major national bank, I earned a reputation as "the go-to guy" to get troubled projects out of the ditch. When you walk into a troubled project, stress levels are already very high. Usually, you have to apply even more pressure to get the project back on track. In spite of that, I am pleased to know that 96% of the people who have worked with me on projects in the past, even troubled projects, are ready and willing to work with me again. I attribute that to stressing people only as much as I must, and being the kind of leader that people are willing to follow again and again.

Developing your leadership abilities is part of the 20% that will give you 80% of your results.

## 3) MANAGE YOUR OWN STRESS

# The Art of Project Management

> "Stress is the mental confusion caused when the mind overrides the body's basic desire to choke the living crap out of some jerk who desperately deserves it."
>
> Anonymous

The job of a project manager is full to overflowing with stress. If you fail to manage your own stress response, you will eventually disintegrate. Either you will collapse, physically, mentally, emotionally, or all three. Or, you will explode, losing your cool and becoming a screaming, raging mess, saying and doing things that will forever damage your reputation and your career.

One of the best ways to manage your stress as a project manager is to become expert in the science of project management. Most specifically, your stress level will go down dramatically if you build project plans which accurately register the interdependence of the tasks so that you are totally aware of your critical path and what affects it.

I discovered this by accident.

I was working as a project manager and enrolled Western Carolina University, earning a Masters of Science degree in project management. One assignment required us to take an existing project and build the project plan fully incorporating task dependencies to reveal the critical path.

For the assignment, I took one of the (then) middling-size projects that I was managing and pretended that I didn't already have a plan. I rebuilt the project plan from the ground up, using my knowledge of the project and tasks, and I took the time to ensure that all my tasks had appropriate successors and predecessors. When I was done, I felt like the fellow in the TV commercial for V-8®, slapping his head and saying, "I could have had a V-8" [instead of whatever lesser drink he had just consumed].

I had worked this project for months, dealing with delays in some tasks and constantly stressing over whether or not an individual slip was going to adversely affect my end-date. As soon as I completed the required exercise, I not only could clearly see my critical path, I could also see what slack I had. From that moment on, I was able to rest easy with this project. I knew exactly how much each part of the project could slip before it caused me issues. That allowed me to ensure that I kept the appropriate pressure on the critical tasks so that they were all delivered on time.

You could say, that was the day I "got religion" about that part of the science of project management. Since then, no matter how painful an exercise it may be, I make sure I record the correct task dependencies in my plan so that I can be consciously competent when managing my project schedule risks. The stress reduction that I get as a return from this investment is immense.

Many project managers pay lip service to the concept of the critical path. The skillful project manager is religious about identifying all the paths of the project. S/he does this not only to reduce risk to the project, but to reduce their own stress.

Aside being an expert in the sciences of project management, knowing yourself is again a key in managing your own stress. I recognize the signs that I am becoming stressed and anxious. I identify the triggers that escalate my stress. I identify deliberate, non-destructive, actions I can take to release tension. You must do the same for yourself.

People don't come with maintenance manuals like you receive when you buy an expensive piece of equipment. There are no engineering studies for people that can mathematically predict the mean time to fail (MTTF) and the mean time to repair (MTTR) for you or anyone else. If there were, we could take the same precautions and preventative measures with people that we do other expensive resources in order to prevent catastrophic failures.

If you aren't getting what I am saying, it is this simple. You put oil in your car every 3,000 miles (as the manufacturer recommends) because if you don't, your engine will break down and leave you stranded. And, the repair bill for a seized engine is enough to push you to buy a whole new car. Unfortunately for you, a regular oil change isn't going to help keep you from collapse.

I could list out a number of things you can do to increase your stress tolerance and reduce your stress. However, although regular exercise and an healthy diet work for everyone, your exercise and diet regimen will likely be far different than mine. Likewise the particular actions I take to manage my stress may be less effective for you than for me.

The bottom line for managing your stress is this – figure out what stresses you and how to alleviate that stress, or it will literally kill you before your time.

Managing your own stress levels is part of the 20% of the art of project management that will enable you to achieve 80% of the results you want.

© Copyright 2017 by @ choreograph, Image used with permission through DepositPhotos.com

## RELEVANT READING

– OR –
A short self-study curriculum in
the Art of Project Management

"**If we encounter a man of rare intellect, we should ask him what books he reads.**"

Ralph Waldo Emerson

If you are reading this book in electronic format, you can click on the resource titles below and be taken directly to the Amazon.com page where the resource is offered. If you are reading a hard copy, you will need to look each of these up on your own. In the interests of full-disclosure, when you use the links below and actually buy the resource, the vendor will send me a small portion of the purchase price. Regardless of the affiliate program rewards, with few exceptions, I have read and applied the resources I am recommending below (and many others besides).

# The Art of Project Management

<u>The Black Book of Executive Politics</u> by Z -This rare little book has some very interesting and unusual information.

<u>The Little Brown Book of Corporate Advancement</u> by Nicholas Noyes – a cynical and sometimes humorous look at some tactics and pitfalls surrounding any conscious efforts at climbing the corporate hierarchy. If you are serious about climbing the corporate ladder, I refer you back to <u>The Black Book of Executive Politics</u>, which is a 100% serious approach to this topic.

<u>How to Win Friends and Influence People</u> by Dale Carnegie. – This classic book about how to charm people is still an inescapable lesson manual in how to deal with people. Ignore it at your own peril.

<u>The 48 Laws of Power</u> by Robert Greene – Robert Greene does an excellent job of elucidating the laws of power and giving meaningful examples. The reader, however, must decide for him or herself what kind of person you want to be. Because if you embrace this book as your guiding light to power, you will become a person who is not very nice or trustworthy. So, read these laws for understanding of what may be happening around you. Then selectively apply them as you see fit to bring about the results (and person) you want.

<u>The Prince</u> by Nicolo Machiavelli – Much like the 48 Laws of Power, Machiavelli's writings are illuminating. However, if you embrace them as your guiding light in life and work, you will become a person who is not trustworthy. When reading The Prince and The 48 Laws of Power, you should consider that just because you know how to fire a gun does not mean that you should shoot whatever crosses your sights.

<u>The Law of Success</u> by Napoleon Hill – Napoleon Hill is most well known for his classic book Think and Grow Rich. This book explains in more detail the principles which underly much of what you find in Think and Grow Rich. Although this too is

a loaded gun, Hill adds a safety with his explanation of what the Golden Rule really means. His notation that we reap what we sow should be kept firmly in mind when considering the use of the materials learned from Machiavelli and Greene.

*Influence: The Psychology of Persuasion* by Robert B Cialdini – Cialdini does an excellent job of explaining various influencing strategies and tactics. Beware that knowing them does not necessarily make you less susceptible to them – which proves their power.

*Managing at the Speed of Change* by Daryl R Conner – The author exposes the most basic factors affecting the ability of individuals to accommodate change. When extrapolated to the organization, it makes extremely useful reading to understand how change is going to work both for and against your efforts as a project manager.

*Built to Last: Successful Habits of Visionary Companies* by Jim Collins and Jerry Porras, the authors draw upon a six-year research project at the Stanford University Graduate School of Business. They took eighteen truly exceptional and long-lasting companies and study each company in direct comparison to one of its top competitors. They examine the companies from their very beginnings to the present day -- as start-ups, as midsize companies, and as large corporations. Throughout, the authors asked: "What makes the truly exceptional companies different from other companies?"

*Getting to Yes: Negotiating Agreement Without Giving In* by Roger Fisher and William L Ury – These two authors manage to cut away the noise around negotiating tactics and expose the bones of the principles beneath it all. Understanding both the principles and the tactics will take your negotiation skills to the next level.

*The Critical Chain* by Eliyahu M. Goldratt – the author uses a novel format to breathe life into the otherwise dry topic of one of the most important pieces of the science of project management which many project managers never truly understand or incorporate into their own (struggling) projects.

*The 7 Habits of Highly Effective People* by Stephen R Covey – This classic book on how to make yourself more effective in your interactions with others is a must read for anyone who truly aspires to lead and motivate people.

*The Art of Project Management* by Scott Berkun – Written in 2005, this book reads like a project management text from the 1990s. There is a lot of valuable material here. However, it intermingles both the science and the art of project management.

While it is true that project management is not warfare, it is typically rife with conflict and opposing forces. Understanding principles of effective warfare can be a very helpful way to gain a new perspective on the struggles of project management and how to deal with the various political maneuvers which project opponents will use to derail your project. Hence, the next two recommendations:

*Principles of War* by Carl Von Clausewitz. The author is perhaps most famous for stating that war is politics carried out in another arena. Applying this notion to the business world, you might say that personal attacks on you by others is just office politics carried out in another arena.

*The Art of War* by Sun Tzu. This ancient classic from China is the source of the quote, "Know your enemy." The advice he gives on how to handle opponents in war are readily adaptable to the world of business. Witness – the number of business leadership courses for which Sun Tzu is required reading.

# LEADERSHIP RESOURCES

*Getting Things Done When You Are Not in Charge* by Geoffrey M.

Bellman. This book is a wonder primer on leading from the middle.

*Good to Great: Why Some Companies Make the Leap…And Others Don't* by Jim Collins. This book is all about leadership and what it takes to be a truly great leader in business. The author studied truly successful, contemporary business leaders to distill critical lessons for leadership.

*Social Intelligence: A Practical Guide* by Johnny Bell. Are you a successful leader? Do people understand what you need from them? Do you fuel an environment of creativity and understanding? With greater social intelligence, you can truly magnify your leadership abilities. You can achieve greater respect, and you can achieve greater output from your employees.

*Emotional Intelligence: Why It Can Matter More Than IQ* by Daniel Goleman. Everyone knows that high IQ is no guarantee of success, happiness, or virtue, but until Emotional Intelligence, we could only guess why. Daniel Goleman's brilliant report from the frontiers of psychology and neuroscience offers startling new insight into our "two minds"—the rational and the emotional—and how they together shape our destiny.

## COMMUNICATIONS RESOURCES

*Crucial Conversations Tools for Talking When Stakes Are High* by Kerry Patterson, Joseph Grenny, Ron McMillan, and Al Switzler.

*Body Language: Secrets of Master Communicators* 10 Instant Download Videos Of Robert Phipps Body Language Training Seminar. More Than 11 Hrs Of Training From One Of The World's Leading Authorities A Complete A-z Guide To Using Body Language.

*How to Read a Person Like a Book* by Nierenberg and Calero. Learn what your friend, lover, boss are really saying to you, but in the language that everyone uses and no one speaks – body language.

*Communication: 4 Manuscripts - Body Language, Small Talk, Public Speaking, Influence (Communication Tools, Communication Skills, Communication For Beginners, ... Small Talk, Influence Book 3)* by Ian Berry. If you want to be one of the most successful people who can leave a good legacy, then being influential and persuasive is something that you ought to develop. Both these traits will allow you to affect the actions, opinions and ideas of others. This makes them not only valuable managerial skills, but also extremely useful in highly collaborative organizations. This is a collection of four essays for beginners covering, Influence, Public Speaking, Small Talk and Body Language.

*Communication Skills for Dummies* by Elizabeth Kunke. Great communication skills can make all the difference in your personal and professional life, and expert author Elizabeth Kuhnke shares with you her top tips for successful communication in any situation.

Packed with advice on active listening, building rapport with people, verbal and non-verbal communication, communicating using modern technology, and lots more, Communication Skills For Dummies is a comprehensive communication resource no professional should be without!

## *The Top Five Assertiveness Books from Amazon*
- Assertiveness: How to Stand Up for Yourself and Still Win the Respect of Others by Judy Murphy
- The Assertiveness Workbook: How to Express Your Ideas and Stand Up for Yourself at Work and in Relationships by Randy J. Paterson
- Boundaries: When To Say Yes, How to Say No by Henry Cloud and John Townsend
- The Assertiveness Guide for Women: How to

- Communicate Your Needs, Set Healthy Boundaries, and Transform Your Relationships by Julie de Azevedo Hanks and Riane Eisler
- Assertiveness for Earth Angels: How to Be Loving Instead of "Too Nice" 4th ed. Edition by Doreen Virtue

<u>The Top Five Assertiveness Audios from Amazon</u>.
- Born to Win by Zig Ziglar
- The Art of Public Speaking by Dale Carnegie and J. Berg Esenwein
- Maximum Confidence: Ten Secrets of Extreme Self-Esteem by Jack Canfield
- How to Develop Your Personal Mission Statement by Stephen R. Covey
- The Success Principles(TM) - 10th Anniversary Edition Low Price CD: How to Get from Where You Are to Where You Are to Where You Want to Be by Jack Canfield and Janet Switzer

# PERSONAL BRAND MANAGEMENT RESOURCES

<u>A Winning Brand: How to Build a Powerful, Personal Brand in Today's Modern, Digital World b</u>y Kraig Kleeman. "Separate yourself from your competition and create a personal brand that matters. Kraig Kleeman and his new book A Winning Brand will show you how."

*Brian Tracy,*
*Professional Speaker and Best Selling Author*

<u>Personal Branding For Dummies</u> By Susan Chritton. Personal Branding For Dummies, 2nd Edition, is your guide to creating and maintaining a personal trademark by equating self-impression with other people's perceptions. This updated edition includes new information on expanding your brand through social media, online job boards, and communities, using the tried and true methods that are the foundation of

personal branding. Marketing your skills and personality, and showing the rest of the world who you are, gives you a competitive edge. Whether you're looking for your first job, considering changing careers, or just want to be more viable and successful in your current career, this guide provides the step-by-step information you need to develop your personal brand.

*The Brand Called You: Make Your Business Stand Out in a Crowded Marketplace* by Peter Montoya and Tim Vandehey. this step-by-step guide for professionals looking to develop a strong company brand has become an international sensation, selling more than 65,000 copies worldwide and hitting #3 on Japan's business bestseller list. This invaluable guide teaches you the vital principles and skills of personal branding, including how to craft an emotionally resonant branding message, create top-quality branding tools, and attract a constant flow of business.

"Montoya's Personal Branding ideas are going to change how business owners and professionals promote themselves."
Robert G. Allen and Mark Victor Hansen, coauthors,
*The One-Minute Millionaire*

*Reinventing You: Define Your Brand, Imagine Your Future* By Dorie Clark A step-by-step guide to reinventing you... Are you where you want to be professionally? Whether you want to advance faster at your present company, change jobs, or make the jump to a new field entirely, the goal is clear: to build a career that thrives on your unique passions and talents. But to achieve this in today's competitive job market, it's almost certain that at some point you'll need to reinvent yourself professionally.

Consider this book your road map for the next phase of your career journey. In *Reinventing You*, branding expert Dorie Clark provides a step-by-step guide to help you assess your unique strengths, develop a compelling personal brand, and ensure that others recognize the powerful contribution you can make. Mixing personal stories with engaging interviews and examples from well-known personalities—Mark Zuckerberg, Al Gore, Tim Ferriss, Seth Godin, and others—*Reinventing You* shows how to think big about your professional goals, take control of your career, build a reputation that opens doors for you, and finally live the life you want.

*Career Warfare: 10 Rules for Building a Successful Personal Brand on the Business Battlefield* by David D'Alessandro. "A refreshing message . . . from someone who has fought many corporate wars."

**The New York Times**

With the latest stories from D'Alessandro's neverending collection of corporate derring-do and new insight on the global battlefield, the nationally bestselling *Career Warfare* is more essential than ever when navigating your way to success.

"D'Alessandro dares to speak the truth. If you don't manage your own reputation, those around you will. This is no theoretical exercise. In corporate America, people talk about you every day. You can affect what they say.

"With a cut-the-crap sharp eye for the passions, yearnings, and follies that drive every organization, D'Alessandro draws apart the drapes and reveals what it really takes to get ahead in business."

**James Carville**,
author and Democratic Strategist

"With good jobs becoming harder to find, D'Alessandro's sage advice is more timely and important than ever, especially for those who are trying to build their personal brands and enhance their careers at the same time."

**Tom Neff**
Chairman
U.S., Spencer Stuart

"Smart, strategic, and useful career advice from someone who has actually achieved success in the real world."

**Harvey Mackay**
author of the #1 New York Times bestseller
*Swim With The Sharks Without Being Eaten Alive*

# OTHER RESOURCES

CareerTrack & Fred Pryor I have personally attended many seminars from CareerTrack and Fred Pryor (*www.pryor.com*). In addition, I have bought many of their audio courses and found them to be a consistent source of excellent training and information. Their topics range from skills training in computer software all the way through supervision, project management, communications, leadership, and management skills.

ToastMasters International (*www.Toastmasters.org*). Toastmasters International is a world leader in communication and leadership development with more than 345,000 memberships. Members improve their speaking and leadership skills by attending one of the 15,900 clubs in 142 countries.

The world needs leaders. Leaders head families, coach teams, run businesses and mentor others. These leaders must not only accomplish, they must communicate. By regularly giving speeches, gaining feedback, leading teams and guiding others to achieve their goals in a supportive atmosphere, leaders emerge from the Toastmasters program. Every Toastmasters journey begins with a single speech. During their journey, they learn to tell their stories. They listen and answer. They plan and lead. They give feedback—and accept it. Through a community of learners, they find their path to leadership.

*A Guide to Self-Directed Learning* (article) by Tom Sheppard available on Amazon.com. This simple, one-page article provides a guide for your self-directed learning efforts.

## ABOUT THE AUTHOR

In addition to his career in corporate America and as a real estate entrepreneur, Tom Sheppard has invested more than a dozen years helping people to get the jobs they want. He has worked on both sides of the job interviewing table: interviewing and hiring job candidates, and coaching job seekers in how to prepare their resumes, conduct job searches, write cover letters, and handle job interviews.

He has taken many of his hard-earned lessons and poured them into his books for job seekers.

On the real estate front, he has invested a lot of time and money in recent years into real estate and becoming a real estate entrepreneur. He has gone from being an award-winning student of some of the most successful real estate gurus in the world to working behind the scenes with more than one.

Many students of the leading real estate gurus seek Tom out to get the "real" story behind a guru or a strategy a guru is teaching.

A former missionary and a U.S. Marine, he has survived and prospered in corporate life, rising to a six-figure salary before starting his own business.

Two Master's degrees and a lifetime of learning as well as a 30-plus-year marriage have taught Tom what it takes to succeed at work, life, and business. In his life, he has swept floors for a living as well as leading teams of hundreds of highly paid executives to deliver multi-million dollar projects on time and under budget for a Fortune 500 company.

In his books, Tom writes about what he knows. If he shares

theory, it is theory that he has tested and proven in his own life and with others. He is adept at taking a complex idea and making it easily understandable.

Tom is sometimes controversial, occasionally outspoken, and always honest.

He is an engaging speaker, mentor, and teacher. He brings his life experience to bear to deliver practical, working solutions to problems that people face every day. He knows that one of the biggest things that holds people back from succeeding is the mistaken belief that it cannot be done in this place or at this time. His experience shows otherwise.

# OTHER TITLES BY TOM SHEPPARD

**Fiction**
If you like to read Science Fiction / Fantasy, here is a trilogy from Tom Sheppard that brings together magic and nanotechnology to tell the 'true' story of the origins of the conflict Tolkien documented in The Lord of the Rings.
- *Origins: The Masterless Sword Book 1*
- *Rise of the Master Mage: The Masterless Sword Book 2*
- *Queen of the Wildwood: The Masterless Sword Book 3*

**Coming Soon:** The Three Sisters Trilogy
- *Seren's Story: Three Sisters Beginning* (Available Now)
- Three Sisters' Courtship
- Three Sisters and the Boy King
- Three Sisters' Second Chances

**Career Management.**
*Fire Yourself: Get the Job You Want a No BS Guide* - DON'T READ THIS BOOK unless you want to TAKE CONTROL of your career, DOUBLE YOUR INCOME, and LIVE THE LIFE YOU WANT.

*Acres of Diamonds (Annotated)* - discover the fortune in opportunity in your own neighborhood or town.

*Career Insurance* reveals how important education is to a successful career. Learn what you need to know to get and keep the job you want regardless of what is happening in the job market. The author successfully used these techniques to go through layoffs, mergers, and acquisitions while growing his paycheck and not suffering from a single day of unemployment for more than 25 years.

*Come Out On Top: Goals To Live By (article)* – Setting written goals magnifies your performance. This article (about 3,500 words) will help you learn how to set challenging, but attainable goals that will change your life.

*Your Career - Your Business: Using Small Business Tactics to Successfully Manage Your Career* - If you want to get and keep the job you want, you need to change how you think about your career and your job. This article (approx. 4,000 words) will change how you think about your career. Instead of relying on others or just thinking about your career as a series of jobs, it will teach you how to look at yourself as a 1 person business and to use small business tools to boost your career to where you want it to go.

*A Guide to Self-Directed Learning* – This short (1 page) guide gives you a checklist to help you with your self-directed learning plan. This plan is part of your larger effort to ensure you get and keep the job you want.

*Start Your Own Business to Have Fun, Make and Save Money* will give you the basics you need to figure out how to turn what you love and are good at into a small business and then use that business and the tax code to save money and make money in your spare time.
- *The Job Hunter's Primer: Get and Keep the Job You Want Vol 5*
- *Tips for Effective Job Searches: Get and Keep the Job You Want Vol 1*
- *Tips for Effective Resumes: Get and Keep the Job You Want Vol 2*
- *Tips for Effective Cover Letters: Get and Keep the Job You Want Vol 3*
- *Tips for Effective Interviews: Get and Keep the Job You Want Vol 4*

## Real Estate Investing

*Millionaire Liar: What the Gurus Won't Tell You About Making Your First Million in Real Estate (but Tom will)* explains and debunks 9 common myths that real estate gurus use to lure you into giving them thousands of dollars. Wouldn't it be better to invest a few dollars in a truth-telling book before you invest hundreds or thousands?

- *Seller Finance for Sellers: The Ultimate Guide*
- *Seller Finance for Buyers: The Ultimate Guide*
- *Market Your House Better Than An Agent*
- *5 Things Every Homebuyer Should Know Before Signing a Contract (article)*
- *5 Ways to Buy a House Without a Bank Loan*
- *Buy a House at 70 Cents on the Dollar: How to Buy Your Home or Investment Property Below Market Value*
- *How to Price Your House to Sell (Article)*

## Politics and Religion

*Godvernment: Government as God* - The two topics you should never discuss at family get togethers, religion and politics brought together in one book, sure to offend almost everyone.

## Blogs by Tom Sheppard

*CareerInsurance.org* – Helping you get and keep the job you want and helping recruiters to better help job seekers.

*BuyBelowMarketHomes.com* – a blog for home buyers and sellers, especially real estate investors.

*MyGodandGovernment.com* – Politics and religion and how they interact in the US.